Walks
on
Shetland

Walks
on
Shetland

by

Mary Welsh

Maps and illustrations by
Rosemary Harward

Westmorland Gazette, Kendal, Cumbria

First published 1995

ISBN 0 902272 94 2

© Westmorland Gazette, 1995

Published by
Westmorland Gazette
22 Stricklandgate, Kendal, Cumbria

Printed by
Craven Herald & Pioneer
Skipton, North Yorkshire

Foreword

Mary Welsh's excellent book will help you discover the delights of our islands. Shetland was made for walkers. It is also an exciting new destination awaiting discovery by those with a sense of adventure and an appreciation of nature.

With almost 1,000 miles (1,600 km) of coastline, the opportunities are enormous, with many treasures along the way. A coastal walk can combine dramatic cliff scenery, long headlands, geos, secluded beaches, wicks, bays and voes — and the prospect of spotting seals, otters and porpoise, as well as the impressive seabird colonies.

Not only can you enjoy the exercise on a Shetland walk, as Mary's book shows you, you can discover archaeological sites, profusions of wild flowers, nature reserves, geological features, birds and mammals, peace and tranquillity, and spectacular scenery.

There are over 100 islands, each one with an individual character. Islanders are naturally friendly and will be pleased to tell you about their way of life, as well as the attractions and delights of their special island. Access to the islands is also easy, with frequent and very economical ferries.

Shetland has something to suit all tastes, whether you prefer an active walk or a gentle stroll. Sensitive and careful walkers are welcomed and we ask you to respect our valued wildlife and not to upset the 350,000 sheep or lambs on our rolling hills.

Enjoy Shetland. If you come as a visitor, please depart as a friend.

Maurice S Mullay
Chief Executive, Shetland Islands Tourism

Acknowledgments

My grateful thanks go to Maureen Fleming, who walked every mile with me, helping in the research and constantly checking and rechecking each route; to Rosemary Harward, whose glorious illustrations and helpful maps must persuade all to seek out the hidden magic of Shetland; to my husband Tom, for his ever kindly support; to P & O Scottish Ferries, for its continued interest and help; and to Maurice Mullay and his staff at Shetland Islands Tourism Information Centre, Lerwick, for their unfailing courtesy and help.

Glossary

Ayre	A gravel beach. Sometimes the name given to a spit of sand and gravel separating a freshwater loch from a voe (see below).
Bod	Once used to house fishermen and their gear during the fishing season. Today it describes basic accommodation for those who want a simple holiday in Shetland. A Hanseatic bod, or booth, was used by Bremen merchants who traded in Shetland.
Broch	An Iron-Age defensive structure.
Burnt mound	A site where ancient man cooked his meat or fish in hot water in a pit. He heated the water by placing hot stones in it and then discarding them as they split.
Chambered cairn	A Neolithic burial site.
Clearance cairn	A pile of stones collected from land under cultivation.
Drongs	Weird-shaped pink granite stacks seen off the north west coast of Mainland.
Geo	A chasm into which the sea flows.
Gloup	A large cave that has collapsed on the landward side to leave a vast chasm.
Hamar	A rocky outcrop on a hillside.
Lade	A channel for diverting water from a burn into the launder (see below) of a watermill.
Launder	A structure, usually wooden, that directed the diverted water in the lade over the paddle wheel which turned the millstones of the watermill.
Noust	A hollow in the turf, at the edge of a beach or loch, just large enough to shelter a small boat from gales.
Plantiecrub	A small stone-walled enclosure where cabbages were grown, safe from sheep and gales.
Scattald	A site from which soil was removed to enrich other areas.
Skeo	A square dry-stone enclosure. The wind blew through the gaps and onto dried meat or fish hanging inside.
Souterrain	An underground chamber, passage, storeroom.
Taing	A headland.
Voe	A sea inlet.
Wick	A bay.

Map of Shetland

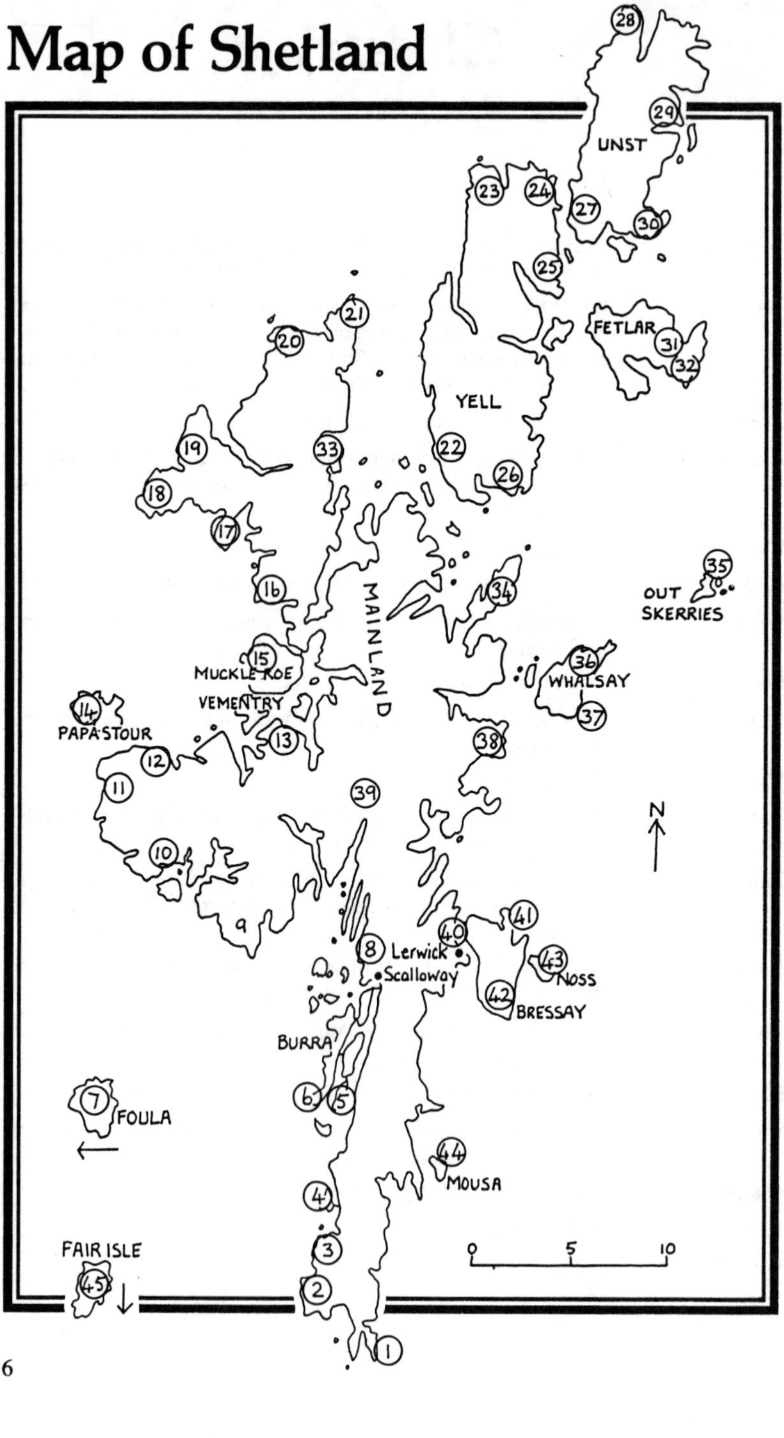
UNST
YELL
FETLAR
MAINLAND
OUT SKERRIES
WHALSAY
MUCKLE ROE
VEMENTRY
PAPA STOUR
Lerwick
Scalloway
NOSS
BRESSAY
BURRA
FOULA
MOUSA
FAIR ISLE
N
0
5
10
1
2
3
4
5
6
7
8
9
10
11
12
13
14
15
16
17
18
19
20
21
22
23
24
25
26
27
28
29
30
31
32
33
34
35
36
37
38
39
40
41
42
43
44
45

Contents

Contents (continued)

1. A Visit to Jarlshof and a Linear Walk to Sumburgh Head

> **Information**
>
> *Distance:* 2½ miles
> *Time:* 2 hours or more
> *Map:* Landranger 4 Shetland, South Mainland
> *Terrain:* Easy walking. A steady, but exhilarating, climb to the lighthouse.
> *Parking:* 397097
>
> *A pleasant road walk with good views and many puffins.*

Jarlshof, the unique archaeological site spanning 3,000 years of settlement, is approached through the car park of Sumburgh Hotel, where you leave your car. The site is named after a medieval farmhouse in Sir Walter Scott's novel *The Pirate*.

To reach Jarlshof use the south-bound A970 and continue through the attractive South Mainland to the airport. The A-road continues to Grutness; the road to Jarlshof, well sign-posted, bears right. Near the site, an interpretative centre and museum displays artefacts and reconstructions of the various stages of occupation. The site is open Monday to Saturday, 9.30 am to 6.30 pm, and Sunday 2.00 pm to 6.30 pm. An entrance fee is charged, with the usual concessions.

The remains of Jarlshof, which had been buried under sand, partly emerged after a violent storm in 1905. The site is many-layered, with evidence of occupation from Neolithic times

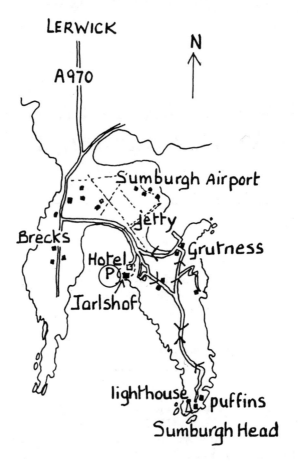

through the Bronze and Iron Ages. The Picts and the Vikings were here, and here, too, a 16th-century laird had his mansion. Wandering through the magnificent ruins is fun for adults and children.

Leave the site and walk round the front of Sumburgh Hotel. It was originally the home of the Laird of Sumburgh and was built in 1867. Continue to the far side of the building and follow the metalled road, which passes between a farmhouse and outbuildings. Look for a drying kiln attached to the latter. Keep on the continuing track to the road, where you turn right. From now on the narrow way leads to the striking lighthouse on Sumburgh Head. This was Shetland's first lighthouse and was

built by the famous Stevenson family in
1821. It is now automated.

On either side of the road, the
sward is covered with wild
flowers. One pasture is a
carpet of pink thrift.
To the right are exten-
sive views of the West
Voe and Scat Ness and
over the Bay of Quen-
dale to Garths Ness
and beyond.

As you near the gate to

Puffins

Jarlshof

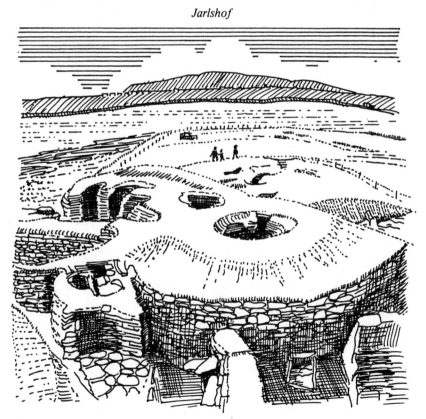

11

the lighthouse, peer with care over the wall on the left to see many puffins by the thrift-covered rabbit holes at the top of the near vertical sandstone cliffs. Look for guillemots in long lines on white rocks, well down the cliffs. Shags, too, nest here in untidy seaweed nests. A large colony of kittiwakes breed on the almost sheer lower slopes and fill the air with their calls. Razorbills can be seen far down. Gannets fly fast out at sea. Fulmars occupy innumerable ledges.

Pass through the gate and again, warily, peer over the wall on the right for another great view of the comical puffins. Wander round the lighthouse buildings and then return along the road. At the track to the farm, taken earlier, you may prefer to walk on to the picturesque Grutness, where you can see the mainland pier for the Fair Isle boat, *Good Shepherd IV.* Continue on the curving road to take the signposted left turn to the hotel car park to rejoin your car.

2. A Circular Walk over Fitful Head

Information

Distance: 5½ miles
Time: 5 hours
Map: Landranger 4 Shetland, South Mainland
Terrain: A stiff climb to the summit. Rather rough walking by the first fence but then good walking on the continuing descent.
Parking: 370120

An exhilarating, demanding walk with tremendous views, plus visits to a watermill and a crofthouse museum.

One of Shetland's highest headlands, Fitful Head dominates the very green fertile Quendale Valley. From its summit at 283 metres (934 feet) the views are magnificent.

To reach this high point, leave the south branch of the A970 at the sign for Ringasta and Quendale. Cross the cattle grid at Hillwell and park on the verge or in a large lay-by further on. Walk back to the farm. Beyond, the track climbs the slope to your left. Check with the farmer about walking over his land.

The good track ascends steadily through sheep pasture and brings you to a large grassy hollow, where cattle graze and curlew nest. To the left flows the Burn of Hillwell. You can see skylark, meadow pipit, wheatear and twite. Now begin the next section of the ascending track, through the crowberry, cotton

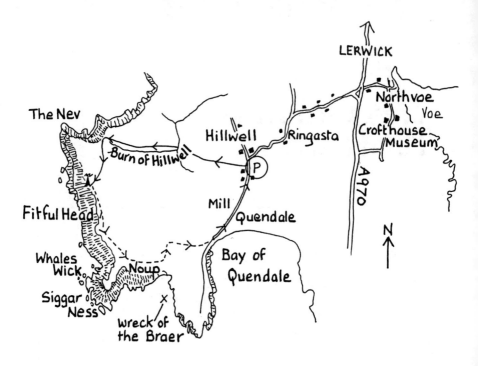

grass, tormentil and heather of North Gill, where oyster-catcher, green plover and whimbrel call. In the wetter areas butterwort, lousewort and pink orchid flower.

At the large bend in the track, take care as you look over the high turf bank to see the ledges of The Nev occupied by fulmars. Continue steadily uphill, now in the territory of the great skua and the snipe. As you climb and climb, pause often to look back at the wonderful view of Loch of Spiggie, Colsay, the Bay of Scousburgh, St Ninian's Isle, and the receding coastline.

At the end of the track stands a huge communications 'golf ball' or radome. Walk on to the gate of a fenced enclosure, within which stands a triangulation point. Cross the fence to the left of the gate and walk round the enclosure to the side of the continuing fence. Press on over the crowberry moorland, keeping close to the fence on your right. Ahead you can see Fair Isle and to the west the island of Foula. Beyond the fence grows a vast area of wood rush. When the fence ends, continue down over the crowberry to walk along the fenced cliffs.

Stride on, steadily descending, with good views of the jagged rocks jutting up through the crashing breakers in Whales Wick. The top of Siggar Ness, which overlooks the Wick, is flat green sward but its sides are almost sheer and fulmars nest among the thrift. Follow the fence as it winds over Noup, a blue haze of squill. From here you can see Noss and Bressay, Sumburgh Head and Scat Ness.

Continue descending. Look right to see the bow of *The Braer,* the American-owned Liberian-registered oil tanker, projecting from the sea. It foundered on Swart Skerry, below Garths Ness, in January 1993, spewing 85,000 tons of crude oil into the sea. Today the water is a turquoise blue and all seems well; the seals peer upwards and a multitude of birds nest.

Walk on down beside the fence. Overhead a pair of ravens soar and wheel at great height. Follow the fence as it turns inland and when you come to a junction of two fences above a very steep slope, cross the fence and descend beside the fence on your right. Drop down the next very steep slope to a flatter area

Ravens over The Braer

below. Pass between the ruins of a large settlement, where a flock of common gulls all sit, tails to the wind, enjoying the sun.

Continue ahead to cross a small burn and walk on to join a reinforced track. This leads to a narrow road, where you turn left. Dawdle beside the beautiful Bay of Quendale, Shetland's longest beach (nearly a mile) where in 1845 more than 1,500 whales were stranded when they swam ashore.

A large raft of eiders float on the turquoise water and house martins skim over the surface of the sea. Walk the road until you reach Quendale Mill, built in 1867 by the Grierson family who owned the estate. It began grinding in 1868. In the 16th century, the estate of Quendale was owned by the Sinclair family. The starving Spanish survivors of the Armada's *Gran Grifon* were brought here from Fair Isle (Walk 45).

The watermill was restored in 1990 and opened in 1993. It has some excellent interpretative panels and is well worth a visit. An entrance fee is charged with the usual concessions.

Continue along the road to rejoin your car. Before you leave this lovely part of the island, visit the Crofthouse Museum at Voe, two miles east, beyond the A970. The thatched crofthouse was built in 1870 and consists of a house, byre, barn, drying kiln and watermill. It is full of authentic furniture and relics of the age, and the peat fire makes you feel very welcome after a blustery walk on Fitful Head. Here, again, an entrance fee is charged, with the usual concessions.

Crofthouse Museum

3. A Circular Walk round Loch of Spiggie

Information

Distance: 5 miles
Time: 2½ hours
Map: Landranger 4 Shetland, South Mainland
Terrain: Easy walking all the way. Can be wet in some pastures.
Parking: 372176

An enjoyable inland walk with a glimpse of the sea from a lovely beach. Some walking on almost traffic-free roads.

To reach Loch of Spiggie, leave the southern part of the A970 at the B9122 and continue to just beyond Scousburgh. The first right turn takes you along the head of the loch, where there is space to park on the left, by a small hut.

The large shallow loch was once a sea inlet, the Voe of Lunabister, but it has been isolated by the natural formation of sand dunes. The lochs of Spiggie and Brow, together with the adjacent marshes, have been designated a Site of Special Scientific Interest by Scottish Natural Heritage. The RSPB owns 295 acres of this pleasant area. The loch is famous for its trout fishing and is also one of the most important in Shetland for its wildfowl.

Of special interest are the whooper swans, considerable numbers of which pass through during their migration south in late autumn. Greylag geese, tufted duck, goldeneye, wigeon,

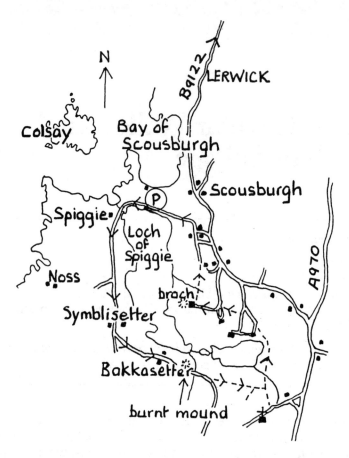

teal and pochard overwinter here. In spring many long-tailed ducks gather to roost and can often be seen displaying. Shelduck, teal, oyster-catchers, curlew and snipe nest in the area.

Start your walk around the loch in an anti-clockwise direction. Arctic terns bathe in the loch. Among them is a wanderer, a white-winged black tern, the white patch on its wings conspicuous against its deep black head, back and breast. Its bill and legs are strikingly red. Nearby a shelduck feeds in a wet gutter unconcerned by the noisy terns. A pair of swallows fly low over the water.

As the road curves, pass through a gate on the right to visit Spiggie beach with its lovely red sandstone cliffs and stacks.

Thrift, sea campion and kidney vetch thrive on the steep faces, and among the natural flower gardens nest numerous fulmars. Kittiwakes breed on the outer lower slopes of the cliffs. Two small rowing boats sit in ancient nousts and there are several more nousts cut into the grassy hinterland of the sandy beach.

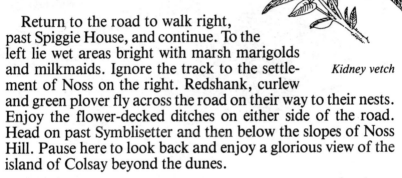

Kidney vetch

Return to the road to walk right, past Spiggie House, and continue. To the left lie wet areas bright with marsh marigolds and milkmaids. Ignore the track to the settlement of Noss on the right. Redshank, curlew and green plover fly across the road on their way to their nests. Enjoy the flower-decked ditches on either side of the road. Head on past Symblisetter and then below the slopes of Noss Hill. Pause here to look back and enjoy a glorious view of the island of Colsay beyond the dunes.

At Bakkasetter look right for three turf-roofed buildings, dating from the 19th century, close by the modern farmhouse. Just beyond, look left to see a burnt mound with two of today's fodder holders in its hollow.

Where the road swings right, pass through a gate on the left to walk ahead, over a pasture, to the next one. Cross over more pastures with Loch of Brow below to the left. Look for an island connected to the land by a causeway of stones, which are now under water. On the green-topped mound, once a broch, 24 pairs of fulmars nest, making good use of a stone sheep pen. Continue to the right of a picturesque ruined crofthouse and some old outbuildings and on to pass through a gate in the wall.

To the right, over the pasture, stands a striking white church with a white castellated tower and red roof, Ringasta Baptist Church, built in 1816. Walk ahead from the gate to the wall of the farmhouse. Here turn left. Head on over the pasture, with Loch of Brow still to your left, to a gate in the wall. Beyond,

Boats in nousts and whooper swans

follow the footpath to cross clapper bridges over two small
burns, where in late spring primroses line the banks. Press on,
diagonally left, to a gate in the wall. Beyond, stride ahead,
keeping to the grassy pasture below the heather. Meadow pipits
and skylarks nest here.

Pass through a gate to the right side of a small house and walk
the continuing metalled road, ignoring the right turn. At the
end of the road pass a low white house with an exquisite garden.
Go through two gates, then walk diagonally right. Pass to the
right of a farm to join a metalled road. Bear left and at the
T-junction turn left again. Enjoy this rural part of South
Mainland, where cattle graze on one side and sheep on the
other. The roadside verges are colourful with flowers.

Continue along this quiet way to the end of the road. Climb a
stile to the left of the house to see the remains of a broch. Look
for the grassy ramparts, part of which have been cut away to
build a modern-day house. In the centre is a hollow in which
would have stood the double-walled tower.

Return to walk right of the house, passing through two gates. Turn right and drop down the slope, with a fence to the right, to another gate. Beyond, walk on to cross a narrow burn and then strike diagonally left, uphill, and pass to the right of a short stone wall that projects into the pasture. Walk through the gate at the end of the wall. There are pleasing views ahead of Loch of Spiggie, Spiggie Bay and Scousburgh Bay.

Keep to the left of a house to join a narrow road and walk on. Pass through the small community of Souther House and at the T-junction turn left to walk beside the loch. Away to the right are the magnificent dunes that have built up to form the wide ayre. Stroll on to rejoin your car.

4. A Circular Walk on St Ninian's Isle

Information

Distance: 3 miles
Time: 2 hours
Map: Landranger 4 Shetland, South Mainland
Terrain: Easy walking.
Parking: 375208

A pleasing walk — a must for all.

St Ninian's Isle, once tidal, is now linked to the mainland by a magnificent shell-sand tombola (isthmus). It is unique, not only in Shetland but in Great Britain, because it is composed of about four feet of sand lying on top of shingle; other tombolas consist only of gravel or shingle. It is a quarter of a mile long and has been built up by wave action from opposing directions — Bigton Wick to the north and St Ninian's Bay to the south.

At each end of the tombola are sand dunes with the associated machair areas, which are particularly well developed at the eastern end. At both ends the dunes have been eroded by natural factors. At the east end sand has also been removed by man.

To reach Bigton, the crofting township that overlooks the isle, follow the A970 south from Lerwick. Turn right onto the B9122 and follow the signpost directions for Bigton. Where the road makes a sharp right turn in the township, look for the

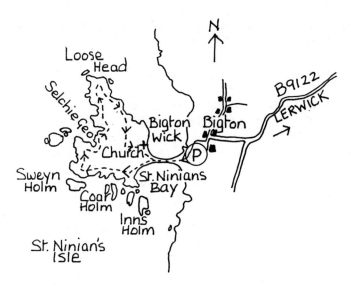

sign directing you left. Drive down the track and park close to the shore.

Descend the continuing track to dawdle across the glorious tombola. Here turquoise water laps gently on both sides. Away to the left is a wonderful view of green-topped islands, stacks and the dramatic Fitful Head (Walk 2). Climb the sandy slope, left, where you can see the roots of marram grass binding the sand. Keep left to begin the pleasing walk around the lovely cliffs. In spring long-stemmed squill grows in great profusion. Thrift, out of the reach *Spring squill* of hungry sheep, lines the cliff faces, together with kidney vetch and sea campion. Buttercups and tormentil thrive and add an extra colour to the pretty sward.

From the most southerly promontory on the island, you can look across to Inns Holm and Coar Holm, each with its ewe and lambs grazing contentedly on the tops, beside great black-backed gulls. When you reach a wall, follow

23

it up the slope to pass through a gate. Return left to the cliff edge and continue on the lovely trek.

On Sweyn Holm, hart's tongue fern thrives. Below, grey seals stare up from the water. Take care at Longa Berg, noticing the hidden edge, and then continue round to Selchie Geo. Look here for puffins preening on ledges, among the fulmars, and then disappearing into the dark crevices of the layered sandstone. Black guillemots nest further down among the rocks.

Walk on towards Loose Head, where more puffins sit on rocks. Overhead two pairs of great skuas circle before harrying any fulmar they can fly down. On some of the rock ledges, well down towards the water, nesting birds call their names, 'kittiwake'. Lesser stitchwort grows among the grass.

Take care as you reach the triangulation point and pause to enjoy the marvellous view. Then begin your return, southwards, where oyster-catchers and shags can be seen and more grey seals. At the wall, walk right to the gate taken earlier. Beyond stroll over the sward to the ruins of the 12th-century church.

It is believed that the site was used for domestic occupation from the first century BC to the third century AD, then as a pre-Christian burial ground where people were buried in a crouching position — short cist inhumation. After that it was probably used as a Christian burial ground, where bodies were placed in long cists and aligned approximately east-west. It is thought that in 800 AD Norse raids might have interrupted the use of the site and that the famous hoard of Pictish silver, referred to below, was buried. Then came Norse Christianity and a larger chapel was built above the first. The chapel was enlarged in about the 12th century. It is believed that the decay of the church came with the Reformation. The island was populated until the 1700s, when peat ran out.

To find the medieval church depicted on maps in 1608 and 1654, the site was excavated in the 1950s. The church had decayed and become totally lost under sand, although the area had continued to be used for burials until the mid-19th century. A gravestone dated 1830 is propped up against a wall.

In July 1958, a Shetland schoolboy was working on the excavation of the site when he found the remains of a box constructed of larch wood. It contained 28 Pictish silver objects, probably a family collection hidden in the church at a time of danger. The treasure is now held in the Royal Museum, Edinburgh, but very fine replicas can be seen in the Shetland Museum in Lerwick (Walk 40).

Walk right from the site to descend to the tombola.

St Ninian's Isle

5. A Circular Walk from Houss, East Burra

Information

Distance: 2½ miles
Time: 1-2 hours
Map: Landranger 4 Shetland, South Mainland
Terrain: Easy walking.
Parking: 377311

A good walk for a warm summer evening.

From Scalloway, drive south along the B9074. Just before Hamnavoe, turn left and continue to Bridge End. Bear left and drive through East Burra to the end of the road at Houss, where there is room to park.

Pass through the gate and walk down a wide grassy track to Ayre Dyke, which is covered with a mass of flotsam thrown up by the tide. Here, among the seaweed, dotterel probe for prey. Pass through the gate and ascend the grassy track with pastures sloping upwards on both sides. At the top you have a pleasing view of Houss Ness ahead. Continue past a ruined croft. From an inlet beside the track, a heron rises, mobbed continually by dozens of arctic terns. On the water a pair of shelduck swim quietly, unperturbed by the drama overhead.

Go on to the end of the fence on your right. Turn right and follow it as it swings towards the shore. Then walk anti-clockwise round the promontory. As you tread a patch of dried

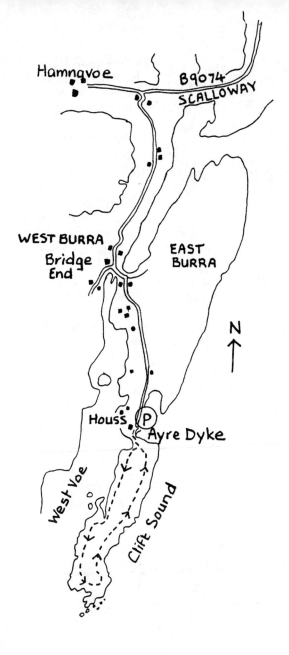

Hamnavoe

B9074
SCALLOWAY

WEST BURRA

Bridge
End

EAST
BURRA

N

Houss

P

Ayre Dyke

West Voe

Clift Sound

South Havra

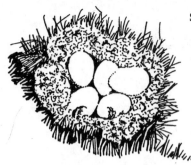

Nest of eider duck

shallow peat hags, walk with care; here an eider has made her lovely down nest and is incubating five large olive-green eggs.

Stroll on along the sheep trods of this pleasing grassy finger of land. Towards the headland, the cliffs become sheer and fulmars, black guillemots and shags have taken up residence. Look for a splendid natural arch. Enjoy a grand view over the sea to the island of South Havra.

Follow the craggy, indented coast round to begin your return walk along the east side. In the shallow water at the foot of the cliffs, a huge forest of seaweed fronds waves back and forth. Across Clift Sound rear the steep grassy Hills of Clift, where mist swirls over the high ridges.

Head on over the grassy way to cross three fences. After the fourth fence, drop down left to cross one more fence to join the track taken earlier. Walk a short distance along the track to cross the ayre. Climb the slope to rejoin your car.

Heron mobbed by terns

6. A Circular Walk from Papil, West Burra

Information

Distance: 4 miles
Time: 2-3 hours
Map: Landranger 4 Shetland, South Mainland
Terrain: Easy walking.
Parking: 368310

A very satisfactory cliff walk with good views.

Take the same route from Scalloway as for Walk 5. Bear right at Bridge End and follow the road as it swings left. The metalled road ends at Papil, where there is ample parking. The name Papil means priests and this was an early Christian site.

Look here to see several ruined crofts and one that has been delightfully restored with a netted thatched roof through which, incongruously, projects a television aerial. Walk ahead along a reinforced gated track. Drop down the hill to cross, on a turf track, a sand and pebble ayre. To the right the turquoise sea laps a glorious white sandy shore. To the left you can see seals basking on the rocks in West Voe.

At the end of the causeway, continue ahead to walk behind a roofless cottage at Minn. Pass through a gate. Press on to the next gate and then to a third, which stands against another ruined croft. Carry on to a gap in the wall and then pass through a gate in a fence onto the heather moorland of Kettla Ness.

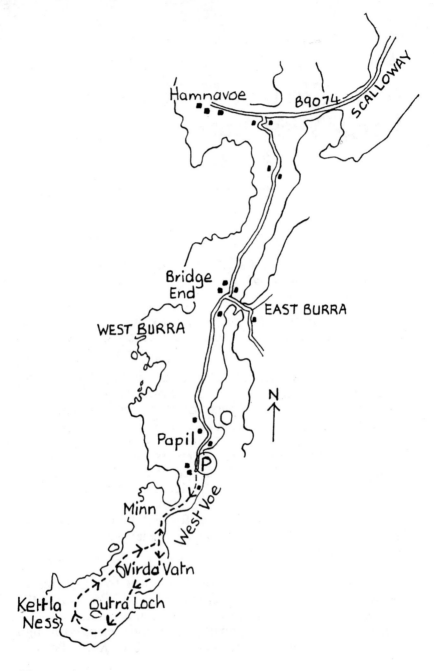

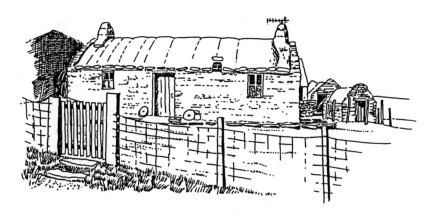

Crofthouse at Papil

Bear left towards the low cliffs, walking over dwarf willow, lichen and heather. From now on follow the lovely coastline in a clockwise direction. To your right, over the bleak moorland, arctic terns dive and wheel, calling harshly as arctic skuas fly among them. On tufts of grass, well separated, great skuas watch. Wheatears call cheerfully as they flit in pairs about the stony areas. Here, too, a trip of dotterel run for a foot or two, then stop, tilting forward to pick up their food. Among them the sociable ringed plovers hurry, uttering their low musical notes. Skylarks fill the air with their melodious songs.

On the shore side, on various pinnacles and jutting crags, sit, separately, many great black-backed gulls, magnificently smart in their nuptial plumage. Several paired birds sit very close. Rows of shags dry their wings on the lowest ridge of a riven headland. Fulmars coo from the many ledges on the steep cliffs. A pair of shelduck, brilliant white and black birds on the wing, fly over the promontory.

As you walk great clumps of thrift brighten the way and among the thin grass violets flower, shading from white to deep purple. Far down on the sea seals swim and further out pairs of black guillemots bob about on the water. Look for natural arches. Gaze at the huge stacks, some grassed on top, others with white campion stretching right down to sea level, and all with birds on ledges and on the top.

As you walk round the end of the headland, there is a spectacular view to the north along the west coast of West Burra. Continue past Outra Loch and then an unnamed one. Stride on to pass Virda Vatn, a larger loch where more dotterel hurry round the shore and a pair of red-throated divers swim.

Carry on along the pleasing way to climb a stile over a fence from where you can see the ayre crossed earlier. Head across a wettish area where numerous arctic terns circle and pass through two gates to reach the causeway. Cross, and climb the track to rejoin your car.

Red-throated divers

7. A Circular Walk on the Island of Foula

Foula is the most westerly island in the Shetland group. It is dominated by high hills and precipitous cliffs. The Sneug, 418 metres (1,373 feet) high, provides a wonderful viewpoint. The Kame, awe-inspiring at 372 metres (1,220 feet), is the second highest cliff in Britain.

To reach this delightful island needs careful planning and the co-operation of the weather. From April to the end of September, Loganair flies to the island on Mondays, Wednesdays and Fridays, allowing between five and eight hours on the island. All these flights are subject to suitable weather. Loganair flies from Tingwall Airstrip on the Mainland, a few miles from Lerwick and Scalloway (telephone 01595 840246). Or you can travel by boat from Walls, West Mainland, each Tuesday returning alternate Thursdays, or every Saturday, weather permitting. Booking is essential (telephone 01595 753232).

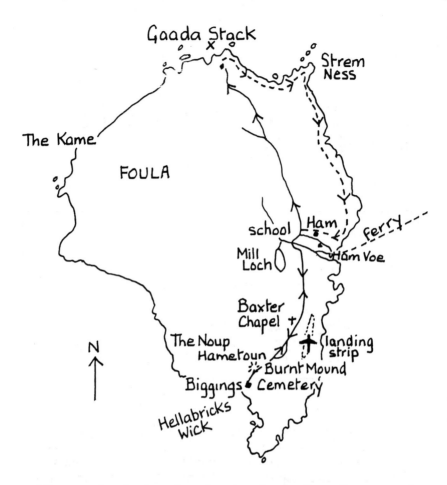

If you go for the day, the adventure begins from the moment you fasten your seat belt and fly down the Tingwall Valley and out over colourful Scalloway, or over green Whiteness and along the west coast. You feel as if you are skimming the waves until you see the gannets, and then the fulmars, below. The boat journey in a sturdy fishing boat takes two hours and is across the open sea where you might see porpoises.

Once on Foula, leave the airstrip with care, for here you are in the territory of hundreds of terns. Their nests, small grassy depressions in the heather, seem to be everywhere and the parent birds are ferocious defenders of their young. Living among the terns are many pairs of arctic skuas who object to any intrusion. Be prepared for mobbing, and wave a scarf, or your hand, above your head.

At the T-junction, turn right to walk the narrow road, to pass Baxter Chapel, which you may like to visit. Stroll on to pass Mill Loch. Here many pairs of great skuas and great black-backed gulls bathe and preen. From the loch runs a tiny stream, lined with marsh marigolds and milkmaids in spring.

Continue through the tiny settlement of Ham, where you will find the post office along a short track on the right. Descend the steep hill and climb up towards the school, which has seven pupils. Here a narrow road comes up from the harbour, the latter opened in April 1990. This is the road you will walk if you travel to the island by boat.

As you continue, notice the many Shetland sheep and lambs, with a variety of colour combinations including the predominating 'moorit' (brown), fawn, grey, creamy white and black. The black and white lambs are particularly appealing. Beyond the school, look for a large sward of low-growing orchids ranging from pink to pure white. In the ditch beside the road, more white orchids grow, together with the pretty purple-flowered butterwort and white milkwort.

Shetland sheep

Gaada Stack

Follow the road as it swings right. As you breast the brow, you have a dramatic view of Gaada Stack, with its impressive natural arch. Continue downhill and then strike left across the pasture, walking through great patches of spring squill and buttercups, to pass Ristie Hostel, which provides simple accommodation for young people. Walk with care as you approach the immense cliffs. Stand here and watch the fulmars flying in and out. Listen for the kittiwakes calling their name to help you detect them nesting lower on the huge cliff face. Watch carefully to see the many puffins returning to their burrows with food for their young. Look for razorbills breeding in crevices on this dramatic rock face. Kittiwakes stream through another magnificent arch.

Return, right, along the cliffs for a closer view of the impressive Gaada Stack and then walk on. Keep above the pebble beach, where great rollers come crashing in. Cross the fence by a stile and then begin the walk round Strem Ness. This is the nesting place of a vast number of shags and some black guillemots. Walk out over the carpet of thrift and look back into the first geo to see the fantastic diagonal patterning of sandstone and schist inter-banded with granite. Notice the intensely weathered cliffs at the northern extremity of this promontory, where a multitude of jagged granite 'teeth' project.

Continue round the glorious coast. Here grey seals peer upwards. One tears a pollock to pieces and the water is red with blood. More peacefully, on the landward side of the path, a mare suckles its foal. Stroll on along the stiled way, with rafts of eiders floating in the quieter waters.

Carry on, still remaining close to the coast. Inland now is a mass of crowberry with some heather, all spangled with tormentil. Here skylarks sing and wheatears nest. This is also the territory of the great skua, possibly the largest colony of this species in the world. Notice the red-throated divers, a pair to each lochan, which have to withstand the predatory birds.

Pass several ruined crofthouses, where the ubiquitous fulmar nests and is rapidly becoming a pest. As you near Ham Voe, spring squill creates a blue haze. Continue outside the fence until you reach the harbour, where you might see the ferry boat lifting off supplies by crane. Walk up the harbour road and turn left.

Press on along the quiet narrow road to pass the airstrip and on to the tiny hamlet of Hametoun. Just before you cross the burn, look for the large burnt mound, Wurly Knowe, a reminder of much earlier settlement of the island. Look upstream of the burn to see the ruins of a watermill and above, on the slope, many ruined crofts. Carry on towards the last house, Biggings, and turn left, just before it, to visit the cemetery with its ruined church and many old gravestones.

Continue to the edge of the cliffs to look over Hellabrick's Wick and right to see the sheer cliff face of The Noup. Walk back towards the airstrip, or to the harbour, where you might see a snipe displaying to its mate, rising in towering circles, 'bleating' as it goes.

A walk on Foula cannot fail to remind you of the derivation of its name from the Norse, *Fugl ey,* meaning bird island.

8. A Circular Walk from Scalloway

Information

Distance: 4 miles
Time: 2 hours
Map: Landranger 4 Shetland, South Mainland
Terrain: Easy walking.
Parking: 405394

A walk with plenty of contrasts.

Scalloway was once the capital of Shetland. It is the second largest settlement and is the major port on the Atlantic coast. Its harbour, full of fishing vessels, is dominated by its ruined castle, which was built in 1600 by forced labour for Patrick Stewart as his principal residence in Shetland. He was Earl of Orkney and Lord of Shetland, a half brother to Mary Queen of Scots. The castle consists of a four-storey rectangular main block with a wing of the same height at one corner. The main block contains a hall at first-floor level, reached by a spacious stair within the wing. The upper floor was divided into a series of chambers. A kitchen and other offices occupied the ground floor.

Patrick Stewart's alleged oppressions have become part of local folklore. It was said that the mortar for the castle was mixed with blood and eggs. He was executed in 1615 and his castle quickly became ruinous. In 1653 it served temporarily

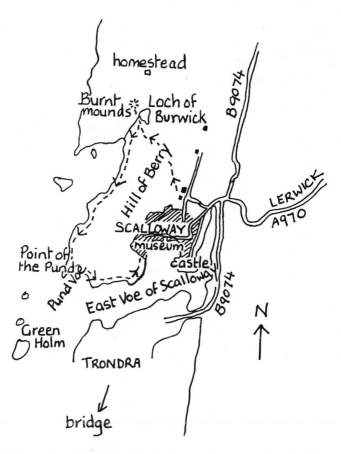

as a garrison for Cromwell's troops. An interpretative display within the castle traces its history.

The key is obtained from close by (see board). With its great dark chambers and multitude of secret corners, it is a great place to visit and a children's paradise.

From the castle, walk along New Street, with the harbour to your left, to pass the Old Haa, once the laird's house. Continue just into Main Street, and on the right visit the Scalloway Museum, which is run by the town's history group. Here you can see fascinating displays on the town's history and, in particular, the 'Shetland Bus' operations during the Second World War; Norwegian patriots in fishing vessels sailed into

Scalloway with refugees and returned across the treacherous waters of the North Sea carrying ammunition and saboteurs.

Leave the museum and walk back the short distance to the corner and turn left. Head along the road past a garden of sycamore, willow, alder, whitebeam and rowan, where blackbirds sing. These trees — a rarity in Shetland — were planted earlier in the century by landowners and prosperous fish merchants. Turn left again to walk beside the wooded area. Then turn right into Berry Road and continue where it becomes a narrow metalled way.

Blackbird on rowan

At a farm, the first dwelling on your left, pass through the gate to walk a reinforced track. Follow it as it swings left and then right round the outbuildings. Pass through the gate and continue to the next. Beyond, walk on, ignoring the track on the left. Ascend the steadily climbing way and pass through the next gate, to where curlew, oyster-catcher, arctic tern and green plover nest.

Once you are over the brow, a splendid view awaits you of the island of Hildasay and many smaller ones. As you descend, look right across to the pretty Loch of Burwick, where bogbean and marsh marigold flower and redshanks nest. Beyond, look for the site of an ancient homestead. Above stands a ruined crofthouse.

Closer to the loch lie two burnt mounds. To visit them, cross the moorland to your right and pass through a small gate in the wall. Follow the small feeder stream of the loch until you come to the two sites. Here, the stream would have provided the water our ancestors needed to cook their meat and fish. Follow the outlet stream as it heads for the sea, and look for the remains of two watermills.

Return across the heather to the gate to rejoin the track. Walk downhill to the bay of Bur Wick. Turn left to cross the wall and begin your walk along the pleasing shallow cliffs. Here flower spring squill, tormentil, milkwort, butterwort, thrift, kidney vetch, hawkbit, violets, primroses, scurvy grass and lousewort.

Out to sea you can see Hildasay where granite was quarried. Black guillemots swim and arctic terns dive for sand eels. The way is generally easy to walk, but care is needed when traversing two small stretches where the cliffs swell upwards.

Pass a ruined crofthouse and stroll on. Ahead across the waters of the voe you can see the houses of Hamnavoe and the lighthouse on Fugla Ness. Then the bridge from Trondra to Burra comes into view.

Cross a new track and continue round the small promontory, Point of the Pund. Stand by the light at the entrance to East Voe of Scalloway and look across to the startlingly green island named Green Holm — an island of limestone, hence the greenness. Scalloway is built on parallel bands of gneiss, schist and limestone.

Walk round the point and across the beach of Pund Voe and continue along the shallow cliffs. Eventually you should leave the shore and walk along the new road towards Scalloway.

At the gated end of the road, turn right towards the shore. Here otters are often seen. Turn left and walk on towards the

Scalloway

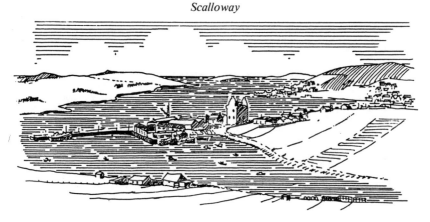

harbour. Pass some old gun emplacements from the Second World War and go on by The North Atlantic Fisheries College, outside which stands a sculpture of flying birds. Pass the boating club, the marina and more sycamores around a substantial house.

Then you come to the Prince Olav Slipway, which was used to repair the vessels of the Shetland Bus operation, and Norway House, where Norwegian seamen lived. The gable end of the house carries a plaque referring to the Shetland Bus. Walk on to pass the museum. Bear right to continue to the castle to rejoin your car.

9. A Circular Walk from Wester Skeld

Information

Distance: 8½ miles
Time: 4-5 hours
Map: Landranger 4 Shetland, South Mainland
Terrain: Good walking, particularly over the close-cropped turf of the cliffs. The short cut at the end of the walk may be too wet after rain, so remain on the road and then take the next right.
Parking: 296439

A lovely quiet walk where you are very unlikely to meet another person.

Leave the A971 by the B9071 at Park Hall, a mile west of Bixter. Follow the B-road through the attractive settlement of Easter Skeld, with its red sands and its pier. A mile further along the B-road turn left, following the signpost for Wester Skeld.

Park near to the Wesleyan Church (1857) and walk on along the narrow road through sheep pastures towards the hamlet of Silwick. Curlews and skylarks call from the moorland slopes of Nounsie. Along the roadside grow flags, butterwort, celandines and marsh marigolds.

Pass a ruined crofthouse built of blocks of granite, a warm pink in the sunshine, and then the sea comes into view. To the left is a sweeping view of South Mainland. At the road end,

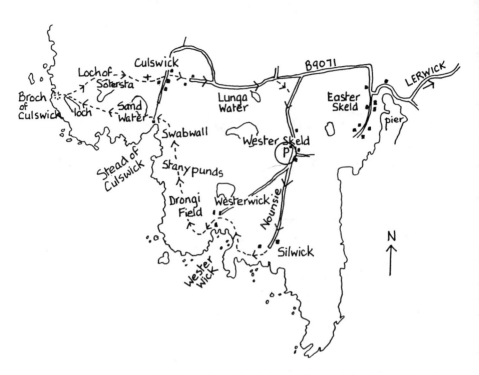

continue on the reinforced track. After a few yards, leave it and bear left to a gate onto the headland where the turf is dotted with violets among large clumps of pretty mauve scurvy grass.

Walk carefully to the edge of the cliffs to look at the astounding view. The deep petrol blue sea turns to white

Sea campion

as it swirls around the jagged, majestic granite stacks of Sil Wick. Fulmars continually leave and return to their nesting ledges on the stacks and on the equally dramatic cliffs. Lesser black-backed gulls chase off a pair of ravens and shags hang their wings — to dry or perhaps to help them digest some rather large portion of food.

Turn right and climb the slope, now with the stacks below to your left. Look for sea campion turning one sheer face to white, and for the pretty thrift dotted among the white flowers.

Stride on the glorious way. Great skuas fly overhead and swallows glide low over the pastures.

Continue on to the spectacular bay of Wester Wick. On an impressive stack in the bay more shags sit. Descend to the tiny valley, where a blackbird sings from the top of a boat shed. Cross the pretty stream lined with great clumps of marsh marigolds. A dark feathered wren flits incessantly over the vegetation, filling the dale with its liquid song.

Climb the steepish slope ahead and walk on, crossing fences as you come to them. Continue over a wetter area, choosing the driest way between peaty pools. From here you have a grand view of Foula, where wisps of cloud tangle with its high cliffs and sometimes its tops peak through low cloud.

Press ahead, slightly away from the cliffs, over the rolling pastures of Drongi Field, Stanypunds and Swabwall. Then descend the steep slope to cross the boulder-strewn narrow beach at Culswick. Pass through a gate on the far side of the beach and climb up the slope ahead to come to the left, or south, end of Sand Water. Here a cloud of arctic terns rise from the loch, screeching as they go. Look for ringed plover probing in the mud of the loch.

Beyond, continue on the steadily rising peaty pastures. Look ahead for your first view of the Broch of Culswick. To reach it, keep left of the Loch of Sotersta, where sheep and lambs graze the bright green grass of a promontory jutting into the blue loch. Look also for a solitary whooper swan idling on the water.

Cross the fence and pass, on your left, a sturdy ruined croft-house with several outbuildings. Stride on towards the broch over more wet ground and then join a newly constructed track on your right. To your left lies a pleasing unnamed loch. Leave the track, left, and head towards the foot of the loch. Cross its narrow outlet stream and the fence beyond, and begin your ascent of the mound on which the broch stands.

On your way up, peer carefully into a very deep geo on your right, where shags nest on ledges halfway down. They call quietly to their mates and these sounds echo eerily upwards. Climb to the broch. It is built of varying sized blocks of granite, some very large. You can just discern two lintels and there are the remains of an outer wall and much of the inner. Sadly, in days gone by, some of the stones were removed to build a sheep pen. Sit on the sward and enjoy this wonderful spot.

Return to the foot of the loch and join the new track. Stroll right (east) for nearly a mile to pass the tiny Culswick Methodist Chapel just before a gate. Here, a notice requests that dogs are not exercised along the track. Continue on the track to the hamlet of Culswick. At the road, turn left. Opposite the post box and before the third croft on your right, pass through a small gate on your right.

Follow the fence on your right down the hillside to a gate. Beyond bear left to cross a tractor bridge over a lively stream. Climb up the slope to walk to the left of a wall and continue along a farm track. From here there is a pleasing view of the valley, golden with marsh marigolds and with the blue bay beyond. Once this quiet valley in the hills would have been alive

Curlews at Westerwick

with the sounds of children, cockerels and dogs, the valley pastures colourful with various crops.

Stroll on along the metalled road and walk up the hill. Ignore the left turn and go ahead, still on a metalled road, over the heather moorland where peats are stacked neatly on either side. Pass Lunga Water, where a pair of arctic skuas sit on rocks, preening after bathing in the loch.

At the next left turn, walk right, keeping to the left of a fence to join a short peat track that cuts off a corner to join the road to Wester Skeld. Turn right and walk on to rejoin your car.

10. A Circular Walk from Walls

Information

Distance: 6 miles
Time: 3-4 hours
Map: Landranger 3 Shetland, North Mainland
Terrain: Easy walking with two steady climbs.
Parking: 244495

A very satisfactory walk along the peaceful coast and quiet roads of West Mainland.

Start from the village of Walls in West Mainland. The name Walls, a corruption of the Norse *'vaas'*, means 'the place of voes'. It is a small village, its sturdy houses spread spaciously around a glorious natural harbour.

Marsh marigold

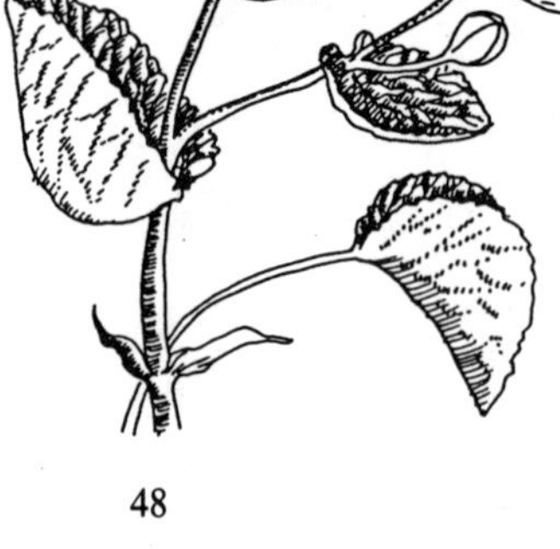

Park close to the garage and the public hall in the middle of the village. Walk south-west to pass the memorial cross on your right. Cross a small stream, bright with marsh marigolds, which leaves the Loch of Kirkigarth and flows into the harbour.

Turn left into Pier Road and continue past the church and the small pier. Where the metalled road ends, walk on

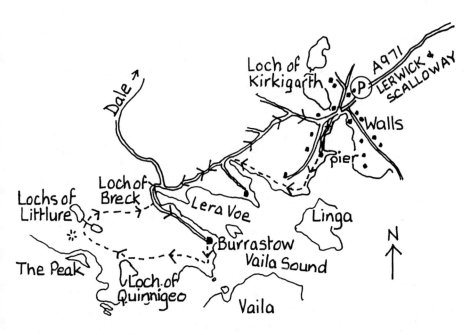

along the reinforced track. Pass through two gates and then bear left along the shore to pass below a bungalow.

Beyond the next gate, look for the ruined chimney on your right, all that remains of a herring station. Look also just above the shore for a noust.

Pass through the next gate and stroll on with a good view to your left of the small island of Linga. Go on to join a reinforced track that leads to a white house at the point. Look over the wall to enjoy the delightful garden, then bear right over the low cliffs, where wheatears flit about the rocky outcrops.

Cross the intervening fences with care and then continue along the shore below a cottage at Stapness. Overhead a great skua swoops menacingly and this sets up a noisy piping from several oyster-catchers.

Follow the edge of a small inlet to see common seals and a pair of eiders snoozing in the sun. Join a narrow road and turn left to walk on. Ignore the next turn on the left and continue. Look for round stone structures, plantiecrubs, where crofters raised their cabbages from seed, safe from the hungry sheep and the destructive wind. On the right, on a green slope, stand the remains of a fine crofthouse, the fresh grass contrasting sharply with the heather and evidence that the land was under cultivation for a long time.

Ignore the right turn to Dale and stride on to the side of Lera Voe. At the head of the inlet stand two small stone buildings, once cornmills, which used water from the loch above to power their grinding. Ringed plovers and redshanks probe among the seaweed on the shore of the voe and overhead a pair of arctic terns call harshly to each other as they dive low over the water. As you walk on, you have a good view of Vaila Sound and the Foula ferry plying towards Walls.

The road ends at Burrastow Hotel, a fine 19th-century house. Bear right just before the entrance gate, keeping to the right of the wall. Continue past the access track to Burrastow Lodge. Pass through the gate ahead and then swing left. Ignore the next gate and walk to the right of the wall. From here you have a dramatic view of the 19th-century baronial hall built by Herbert Anderton, a Yorkshire millowner. Up above the hall, on the cliffs, stands a look-out tower. Legend has it that it was used by the millowner to watch his fishing boats come into harbour, checking that none of his employees dropped off some of their catch along the coast. He wanted all his fish.

Walk on with care along the cliffs to a wall and follow it right until you reach a gap. Beyond, continue with the fence to your right. Here, violets spangle the close-cropped turf. Pass through a gate in the right corner. Pause here to look down on a secluded pebble beach and ahead to a patch of blue between rolling slopes, a first glimpse of the Loch of Quinnigeo. Bear right to walk around the top of the loch.

Climb the fence beyond and walk ahead through heather. Look here for another small cornmill, which drew its water from a small loch on your right. Climb the next fence and begin the steady climb to a cairn on the hill ahead. As you go, look left for traces of a grassy track that would have led to the mill and been well used.

Walls

Pause at the cairn, where a spectacular view awaits. Below, great white breakers crash on the jagged rocks of The Peak. From here you can also see the new reinforced track, which is not on the OS map. Drop down the slope to the track and turn right. To your left and right lie the Lochs of Littlure.

Stride the reinforced way. Pass more plantiecrubs. On your left is Loch of Breck, from where come the wailing cries of a pair of red-throated divers. At the road, turn left to join the road walked earlier. Again, ignore the road to Dale and walk on. Continue where the quiet moorland road climbs and climbs to a T-junction. Turn right to drop down the steepish hill into Walls and to rejoin your car.

11. A Circular Walk from Huxter

Information

Distance: 4 miles
Time: 3 hours
Map: Landranger 3 Shetland, North Mainland
Terrain: Good walking. Steep climb to Banks Head and the cairn.
Parking: 175572

A challenging walk with good views over the jagged coastline and from the cairn on Sandness Hill.

Drive towards West Mainland along the A971. Ignore the left turn to Walls and continue in the direction of Sandness. At the school, do not take the continuing A-road to the pier but drive along a narrow road to its end — Huxter. Park in a small lay-by on the right, just before the dwellings of the tiny settlement.

Walk on, with the cottages to your left, and climb the fence opposite them. Drop down the slope to pass through a gate. Bear left across the pasture to a stream. Here, in a small ravine, are three ruined watermills. Two still have their paddles and one its grinding stones. Each thatched mill would have been shared by two or three families in the days when corn was grown.

Head up the pretty stream, which is lined with marsh marigolds, to a fence. Walk towards a wall and pass through the gate. Climb the stone-stepped stile almost immediately on your

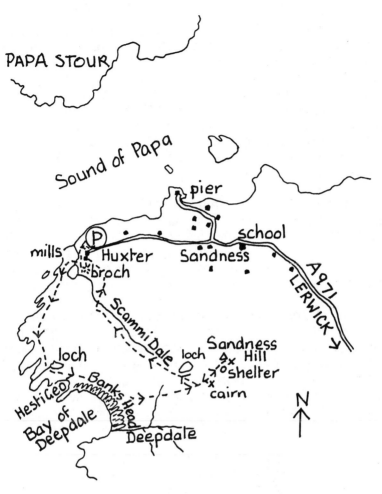

right. Beyond, cross the small stream where it leaves a loch. Stroll round a large stone sheep pen to see the remains of a broch. Look for a lintel still intact.

Return over the stream, climb a fence ahead and stride over the links to walk on along the cliffs, with the great breakers rolling in on your right. Across the Sound of Papa lies the hilly island of Papa Stour.

Continue over the turf, where sea thrift flowers in profusion. Look, with care, over the cliff edge to see the magnificent folding and tilting of the sandstone cliffs and for the volcanic lava that runs in bands through the sandstone. Ahead, the island of Foula, with its dramatic cliffs, appears through the sea mist. Climb a stone-stepped stile over a very long stone wall and stroll on. Pass a loch on your left where two pairs of great skuas idle. Then walk the edge of the Bay of Deepdale. Peer down the spectacular Hesti Geo and then begin to climb. Far down in the bay a series of stacks spike upwards. Climb up and up towards Banks Head, with breathtaking views of the almost sheer cliffs sliding down to the bay.

Climb on. Now you are immensely high and everything that seemed high before is below you. As the great cleft of Deep Dale comes into view, strike inland, following the same contour to avoid losing height. Look here for mountain hares, loping over the pastures. Suddenly one will stop and sit bolt upright, its white ears pointing upwards.

Go on inland to where you can see a tall stone cairn high on Sandness Hill. Head towards it, walking over crowberry, lichen, clubmoss and heather, accompanied by carolling larks and courting curlews. Ascend over a 'sea' of shattered pink and blue stones to the cairn. To your left, in a hollow, lies a small loch. Walk on along the ridge to a stone shelter. Pause here to enjoy the fine view. Ahead lies another cairn and the triangulation point 249 metres (799 feet).

Mountain hare

Return to the first cairn, from where you can see your car parked far below. Drop down to the left side of the loch and then continue to descend steadily over the crowberry, heading to a junction of walls down on the links. To your right lies Scammi Dale. Keep well up the slope above the dale.

When you reach the bottom of the hill, pick the driest way across the intervening wettish area to cross a fence.

54

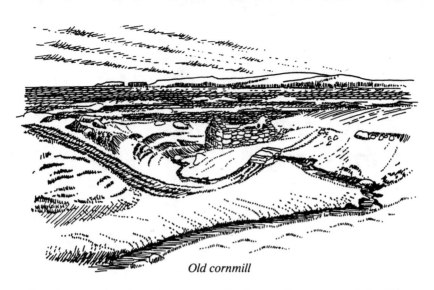
Old cornmill

Continue over the pasture, with the wall to your left. Pass through the next gate to join a reinforced track and follow it to Huxter to rejoin your car.

12. A Circular Walk from Norby

Information

Distance: 4½ miles
Time: 2-3 hours
Map: Landranger 3 Shetland, North Mainland
Terrain: Easy walking.
Parking: 199575

An attractive coastal walk with the return route along a quiet narrow inland road.

Drive along the A971 as for Walk 11. Just before the attractive township of Sandness, take the right turn signposted Norby. Continue down the narrow lane and park on the left, just before it ends on the shore.

Walk to the edge of the shore and turn right along a sandy track where marram grass grows. Offshore, several pairs of eiders call quietly to each other, the males resplendent in their nuptial plumage. Carry on along the edge of the lovely sandy bay, which is called The Crook. To your right, a solitary whooper swan sails on the Loch of Norby.

The Holm of Melby lies offshore and beyond, across the Sound of Papa, is the large grassy, hilly island of Papa Stour.

Step across the narrow stream that exits from the loch and wander along the grassy way. Pass through a gate and stroll

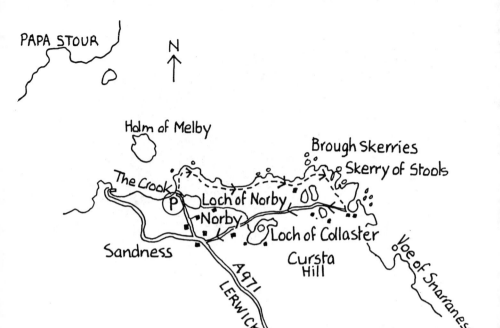

over low cliffs. Continue where the cliffs rear up, taking care not to go too close to the edge. Look for fulmars, which make use of every ledge for nesting. Below, in the water, a single black guillemot bobs about on the waves.

Walk over the closely-cropped turf, with ever-extending views of Papa Stour and North Mainland. Approach the fence to your left and look down to the tiny bay far below. Here, on jagged rocks, several common seals sprawl. Carry on up the slope and climb the fence. Meadow pipits and wheatears flit about the boulders.

From the ridge, look right, down the grassy slopes above the Loch of Norby, to see an extensive carpet of primroses. Overhead, a pair of ravens chase a fulmar, but it outwits them and settles on a ledge.

Continue over more fences. Look down to the left to see two dramatic natural arches, which turn the sea to turquoise and

Norby

white as the waves crash against them. Beyond the next fence, cross over the finely-cropped turf, which is dotted with violets. Pass through a small gate and climb several more fences with care. Remember to look back often to see the dramatic coastline. Look for a cliff face with primroses stretching down to the shore.

Dawdle on and then drop down a slope to a rocky bay where more seals snooze and several, inquisitively, swim close to the shore. Cross a small stream bright with marsh marigolds, celandines and daffodils. Continue past Brough Skerries and the Skerry of Stools. Inland, a bonny loch comes into view. Walk towards it following a stream and look for a ruined watermill built across the hurrying rivulet.

Moss campion

Follow the continuing cliff edge as it turns south to give you a fine view of the Voe of Snarraness. As you swing towards the road, now visible on your right, pass below rocky out-crops. Look here for cushions of the pretty moss campion among primroses. Keep to the right of the cottage to join the road. Pass an almost complete circular bay that has a small exit to the sea. Here several seals swim and peer. Carry on along the road where it swings right, its sides lined with primroses, celandines, marsh marigolds and dwarf willow.

Head on along the way. To the left, lie the moorland slopes of Cursta Hill and close by the road the Loch of Collaster, where terns nest. When you eventually reach the T-junction, turn right and then right again to walk through the scattered dwellings of Norby to rejoin your car.

13. A Circular Walk from Vementry, West Mainland

Information

Distance: 4½ miles
Time: 2-3 hours
Map: Landranger 3 Shetland, North Mainland
Terrain: Easy walking.
Parking: 312596

A delightful walk through heather on a good path, followed by an excellent coastal walk.

This is a glorious walk through the remote countryside west of Aith. Leave Lerwick by the A970. Then take the A971 and continue to Bixter, where you turn right. Pass on your left the attractive settlements of Twatt, and then Aith. Bear left to continue along the west side of Aith Voe, through the peninsula of Aith Ness. Drive to the end of the road. Park in the lay-by on your right, beside one of the Lochs of Hostigates, and just before a cattle grid.

Take the good track going off south (left), beyond a metal gate. Enjoy the delightful way as it passes through heather above the other Loch of Hostigates. Here, a pair of red-throated divers idle, watched by a great skua at the edge of the water. Tormentil and hawkweed thrive among the heather, which, in August, is a haze of pink.

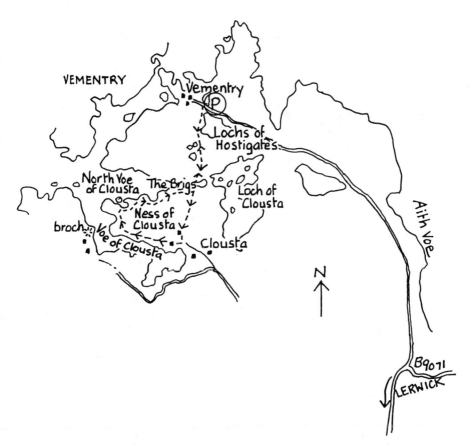

A pair of arctic skuas nest on a small hillock overlooking the path and curlews brood their young close by. Pass two more small lochans surrounded by milkmaids and marsh marigolds. Look for a mountain hare loping through the heather, its tail and underparts white, its ears black edged with white.

Follow the gently ascending path to the brow of the hill and beyond you can see the large Loch of Clousta with its several green-topped islands. Continue downhill through the schist and heather to cross The Brigs, an extension of North Voe of Clousta. Stride the two man-made causeways that cross, depending on the tide, an outlet from the fresh-water loch or an inlet from the sea loch. Here, redshanks fly up from probing the mud, uttering their plaintive calls. On a seaweed-covered rock sit four turnstones, tabby short-legged birds, very black and

Mergansers

white about the head and neck with bright orange legs and a short slightly up-tilted bill. Among the pebbles by the causeway grows Danish scurvy grass.

Continue ahead to walk uphill, where there is no path. Milkwort and butterwort thrive in the pasture. At the brow, you can see the settlement of Clousta below, clustered around the head of the Voe of Clousta. Begin the steady descent close to a colony of terns, passing through gates until you reach the road by the shore.

Turn right. After a few yards, bear left to walk the shallow cliffs of the beautiful, indented coastline of the Ness of Clousta. Spring squill, thrift, milkwort, lousewort, tormentil, kidney vetch and mountain everlasting create a lovely sward. On the water of the voe, two pairs of mergansers squabble over their territorial rights.

Causeway from Vementry

Continue past a ruined wall, plantiecrub and sheep pund. Then, as you round the next corner, you have a spectacular view of the dramatic cliffs of Neeans Neap. Look across the voe to the north side of the last two houses to see a small promontory on which stands a ruined broch.

Stroll on round the final promontory of the Ness and continue with the North Voe to your left. Pass more plantie-crubs and remains of an earlier settlement. Overhead, a pair of ravens glide. Go on towards The Brigs, walking over sundew in the wetter areas. Here you might see an otter.

Recross the causeways and begin the lovely walk back, through the heather, to rejoin your car.

14. A Circular Walk round Papa Stour

To reach the West Burrafirth pier and ferry, leave the A971 at the second turn on the right, if travelling west, after Bixter. The signposted narrow road leads over a wild moorland where oyster-catchers fly and curlews nest close to the road. There is ample parking at the pier and the facilities are excellent. The large sturdy passenger boat, which looks more suited to fishing, takes you through the firth, past its islands, and then across the Sound of Papa. The distance is about one mile and the journey takes 30 minutes. Look for razorbills, puffins, gannets, shags and porpoises as you go.

The ferry leaves at 9 am on Monday, Wednesday and Friday from West Burrafirth and returns from Papa Stour at 7 pm. If the weather is bad, this is a long time to spend on an island that has no cafe, shop or natural shelter from wind or rain, so choose a good day and go well equipped. You are asked to book by telephone; the number to use is 01595 73227. All bookings

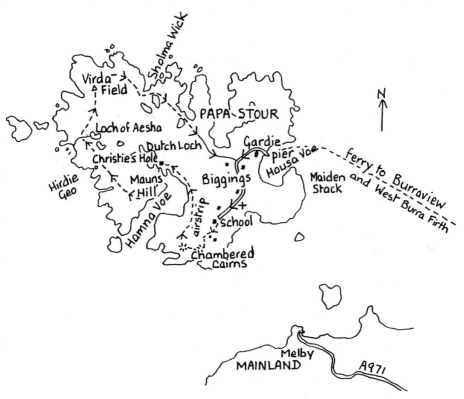

should be confirmed 24 hours before departure. The fare is inexpensive and there are good concessions.

As you enter Housa Voe on your way to dock at the island's pier, look left to see the dramatic red stacks guarding the way.

The pier in West Burrafirth

The largest is known as The Maiden. Legend tells that a young girl, who had fallen in love with a low-born suitor, was confined to a stone house on top of the stack. She was rescued by her ardent lover and eventually, happily, he became an accepted member of the family.

The Vikings gave Papa Stour its name, which means the big island of priests. Celtic priests are believed to have lived here as early as the sixth century.

Walk up the narrow road to pass a roofless house on your left. This is all that remains of Gardie House. Here, in the 19th century, Edwin Lindsay, an officer in the Indian army, was confined for 26 years by his father for refusing to fight a duel. Look on the telephone wires as you walk inland for a small group of twittering twites.

Continue along the road to Biggings until you reach an interpretative panel on your right. A stile gives access to excavations that revealed the foundations of a medieval Norse house. Walk on until you reach the kirk. Go inside and enjoy the peace of the perfect tiny church. Look for the lovely stained glass window, a poignant memorial to those lost in the First World War. The church has attractive wooden seats.

Stroll on to pass the old manse and then the village school. At the time of writing, there was one pupil supported by all the necessary modern equipment. The metalled road ends beyond the gate and continues as a reinforced track to the airstrip, a large barren area with one tiny building. Cross the strip and climb the stile in the fence by a marker post at the foot of the Hill of Fielie. Here, where only stones remain, was housed a leper colony. Nowadays, it is believed that these outcasts did not have leprosy but a disfiguring disease caused by a very poor diet.

Return over the stile and climb up the slope. Cross the fence and then the hill dyke, the dividing line between the open heath and the richer pasture land. Bear left over the slope to Muckle Hoogan to see the waymarked remnants of a 'heel-shaped' chambered cairn, a Neolithic burial site. Sit by the stones and enjoy the view. You can see the route taken on Walks 11 and 12 on West Mainland, and also the dramatic outline of Foula.

Walk right to recross the hill dyke and stroll over the open heath, known as the scattald land. Here the plants are exposed to salt-laden winds, so creep close to the earth. Thrift, thyme, woolly hair moss and rough grass grow among the low-growing ling, providing nesting sites for great and arctic skuas, wheatear and golden plover. You will see many curlews and terns.

Continue to the top of the hill to see another marker post by a group of stones, all that remains of a second chambered cairn. Drop down the slope to climb the stile by the leper refuge. Beyond, walk ahead (north) along the side of the extensive Hamna Voe. Look for many boat nousts along the side of the water, one containing a boat.

By the water, at regular intervals, stand a series of plantie-crubs, several of which have cabbages growing. The tops of the crubs are covered with nets to keep out birds. Stride on around the head of the voe, where a dozen or more young curlews feed on the shore. In 19th-century storms, several ships came to grief on the submerged reefs of the voe.

Continue to a small stream to look for two ruined watermills. One still has its revolving drum intact and the other its wooden launder. This directed the diverted water in the lade over the paddle wheel, which turned the millstones. The stream that provided the power flows out of Dutch Loch above. These mills

A plantiecrub

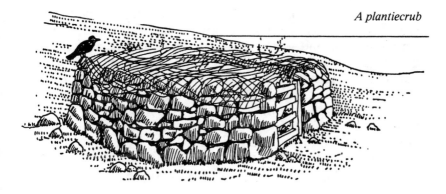

were in use at the beginning of the century. The island once had 24 of them. Dawdle beside the voe, where you might see ringed plover, dunlin and sanderling.

Walk on until you reach the fence. Do not cross but walk up beside it, on your left, to climb Mauns Hill. Continue ahead from the fence over the scattald. Here, top-soil was removed to enrich the fertile eastern side of the island and the resulting heath provides an ideal environment for ground-nesting birds. A vast number of arctic terns scream as they wheel overhead and, if you visit the island during the breeding season, circle this area to allow the birds to tend their broods undisturbed.

Beyond the horizon of the scattald a glorious view awaits of the magnificent west coast. Approach any of the geos, inlets, gloups, cliff edges with great care. North Lunga Geo is most spectacular with its own little stack. Walk right, towards Christie's Hole. Here, a gloup has formed with a wide bridge of land intact between the great hole and the cliff edge. A few yards inland, another gloup is forming. Both are sheer and very deep and give little warning of their presence even on a bright sunny day.

The gloup has been colonised by shags and on ledges, half-way down, they sit on their brilliant white eggs in large untidy nests of seaweed. As their mates approach, they call and the rough sounds reverberate through the deep hollow. Look circumspectly.

Continue, to pass large clumps of moss campion and thrift. Above Hirdie Geo pause and enjoy the natural arches, stacks and wonderful pink cliffs. Look for seals and listen to their eerie wailing. Walk down to the stream, where there are more watermills. Climb upstream and continue with the large Loch of Aesha to your right. Continue over a boulder field to climb to the triangulation point 87 metres (285 feet) in its walled shelter on Little Virda Field. From here you can look along the northern coast, and see nearly all the island with its many lochs. Look out to sea, to Ve Skerries with its lighthouse, built in 1979 after several ships ran into trouble on the rocks.

Drop down the slope and begin to walk east along the indented coastline, past Sholma Wick and The Kiln, the latter a huge waterless hole with a rock arch. Keep to the left of three small lochs, all of which supported watermills. Today a pair of red-throated divers swim lazily on the still waters.

Stroll on to pass on your left The Loch That Ebbs And Flows. Here, a whooper swan swims quietly until it is mobbed by arctic terns and encouraged to move away. The eiders are left in peace by the aggressive birds.

Go ahead to a gate in the fence. Head right to a marker post where there is believed to have been a prehistoric settlement (3,000 BC). Close by are the remains of a crofthouse. Here, pick up a clear causeway, heading east. This is one of the two 'meal' roads to be seen on the island and they were built by labour paid for with a meal during famine in the 19th century.

The meal road is soon lost under a track and this leads towards a gate and a fence. Walk left along the fence to a good stile. Beyond, turn left to walk back to the pier. On your return journey on the ferry, on a calm day, you might be restored by a very welcome cup of tea and oatcakes. At the pier at West Burrafirth otters are often seen and several come aboard the boats in search of fish.

15. A Circular Walk on Muckle Roe

Information

Distance: 6½ miles
Time: 4-5 hours
Map: Landranger 3 Shetland, North Mainland
Terrain: Easy walking.
Parking: 322628

Perhaps one of the loveliest walks on Shetland.

From Lerwick, drive north on the A970 to Brae. Continue round the head of Busta Voe and then take the first left, signposted Muckle Roe. Look left to see Busta House, the laird's dwelling in the 16th century. Go over Muckle Roe bridge where, because of weight restrictions, only one car can cross at a time. Beyond, a notice insists that all dogs must be on a lead at all times, if they are allowed out of a car. Drive on along the metalled road to the end, where there is some space for parking.

Walk the wide gated track, which climbs steadily. Then continue ahead through a valley between Muckla Field and Mid Field. The track has been cut through red granite that is heavily overlaid with peat on which heather flourishes. In places, the colour of the granite has been bleached, and eroded lumps lie beside the way.

Pass a small loch and then several rows of neatly placed blocks of peat. These are cut by hand, using a specially shaped

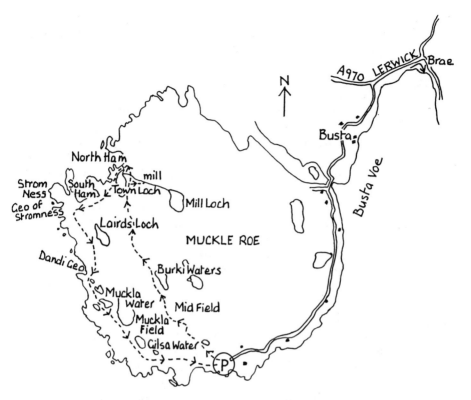

tool called a tushkar. Go on along this sheltered way, which cuts deep into the moorland heart of the little island. Look up on the stunted ling to see plump bullet-headed golden plover with their yellowy downy nestlings, hurrying over the herbage.

Carry on past Burki Water, where a solitary red-throated diver idles. A small stream issues from the loch, passes below the track and then accompanies you to the left. A little further on and you have a glorious view of Town Loch at North Ham, where the valley opens out into a wide flat grassy area. To the right stands a ruined crofthouse and its outbuildings.

Golden plover with chicks

Where the track swings left, walk ahead to a gate and bear right to pass in front of the old dwelling, crossing its once extensive grazing land. Keep to the right side of the loch until you reach a gate. Do not pass through but climb up the slope to the side of a small watermill. It is roofless but still retains a paddle and its millstones. Enjoy this secret hollow where the burn, which has tumbled out of Mill Loch, descends in many pretty falls. It is this stream that was diverted to turn the millstones.

Return to the gate and pass through. Walk beside the fence to your right to pass below the steep-sided gill, through which the burn continues to descend to join Town Loch. Stroll on to the lovely bay of North Ham and here do some summer dreaming. The glorious deep blue inlet is edged with huge red cliffs, stacks and a natural arch. Green and orange lichen grow on the red granite and the colour combination is quite beautiful. Shags, ravens and fulmars make full use of the many ledges, ridges and crags.

Cross the bank of rounded boulders that separates the loch from the sea, and bear left to pass below the end of the fence. Then begin the steady climb upwards with curlews, oyster-catchers, and great black-headed gulls calling as you go. At the top of the ridge, the dramatic coastline lies to your right. Enjoy its many inlets, geos and stacks — but proceed with care. Look for mats of moss campion, ranging in colour from pale lilac to deep mauve. Peer carefully at the sheer sides of geos to see the fleshy-leaved roseroot softening the vertical crevice in the granite.

Pass another ruined crofthouse and drop down the slope to the side of South Ham, where the sand is a warm red gold. Here seals slumber on the rocks and eiders swim. Climb the fence and walk on past more lovely clumps of moss campion. Join the end of a track and take the gate to your right.

Pass yet another ruined crofthouse and cut across Strom Ness. Take great care as you walk round the side of the immensely deep Geo of Stromness. From here, strike up onto the rocky top of the West Hill of Ham. Look for thrifts in flower and for an arctic skua sitting on a heather clump. From the rocky ridge, you can see the low-lying Papa Stour and beyond, in the misty distance, the high cliffs of Foula.

Keep well to the left of Dandi Geo to come to three small lochs. From the nearest one a burn issues and descends in a great fall to the foot of the deep ravine. And then you can see part of Muckla Water to your left. Continue ahead between the two nearest lochs. Walk on over the rough grass and the shattered rocks, passing between the warm pink outcrops.

When you reach the foot of Gilsa Water, follow a narrow, but safe, path along the right side of the loch, where a pair of red-throated divers swim serenely. Climb the slope at the other end and continue beside a small lochan. The narrow path stretches ahead through the heather.

Soon a lovely bay lies far below, its rich red-gold sand turning the water turquoise and then purple. Just when you feel that

Cutting peat

the way is becoming too 'white knuckle', the path is protected by a hand rail and you can enjoy the magic scene below. Continue to a fence, which you cross by a stile.

Dawdle on along the clear path, with another glorious sandy bay below. At a small cairn, begin the descent of the heather cliff to step across a stream to a track. Cross and walk up the other side. Follow the path to join the track, just before the first gate taken at the outset of your walk. Rejoin your car just beyond.

16. A Circular Walk from near Mangaster

Information

Distance: 7 miles
Time: 4-5 hours
Map: Landranger 3 Shetland, North Mainland
Terrain: Generally easy underfoot but plenty of hills to climb
          and descend.
Parking: 335719

*An exciting and challenging walk. Plenty of road walking, but
these roads are narrow and virtually car-free.*

Superb is the only word to describe the scenery from Mangaster
to Nibon on the west coast of North Mainland. A disadvantage
with walking this stretch of the lovely coast is that you have to
return by the same route, unless you either cross an extensive
difficult upland peat bog (not recommended) or you walk for
two-and-a-half miles along a road. However, even the road
route has its compensations: the narrow roads of Shetland are a
pleasure to walk; rarely do you meet cars and, if you do, many
drivers stop for an interesting chat.

Leave Mavis Grind by the A970 and pass Mangaster Voe on
your left. Ignore the next turn on the left, which leads to
Mangaster. Drive on for just over half a mile, to park in the
signposted lay-by on the right side of the road.

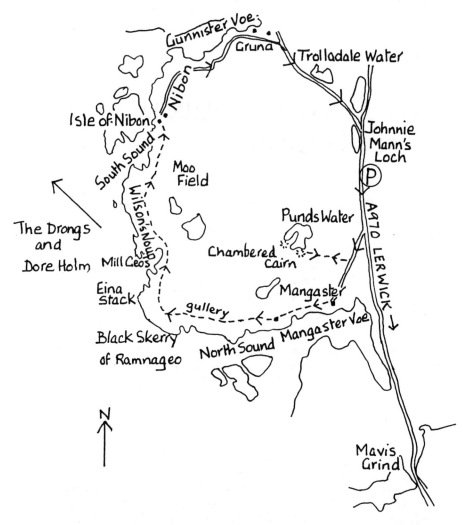

Walk back along the A-road and turn right onto the single-track road to Mangaster. You might like to strike off right, through a gate and climb west to Punds Water, a large kidney-shaped loch. Here, at map reference 324712, above the south shore of the loch, stands a large mound of stones, the remains of a chambered cairn shaped like a heel. It has an entrance passage and the roof has fallen into a clover leaf-shaped chamber. Large white granite boulders form the five feet high wall of the cairn.

Descend to the loch and walk left round it to the start of a projecting spit of land. Here, look for a second tomb, which is almost circular in shape and divided into five small cells — shades of a modern home.

Return to the road and continue downhill to Mangaster, with the large pleasing voe of the same name to your left. Stride on where the road becomes first a reinforced track and then a grassy way. Pass through the gate and stroll through the heather, with a sturdy, well-built wall to your left. Across the narrow North Sound lies a group of very green islands.

As you walk, look left to see Muckle Roe, with West Mainland beyond. Out to sea lies Papa Stour and, far out, Foula. Shags fly up the sound and pairs of eiders fill the air with their pleasing mewing.

Steepish slopes tower above you and more gently-sloping pastures drop down towards the sea. Follow the sheep trods through the heather to come to a delectable bay. Descend towards the burn, which tumbles through a steep gill. The stream originates high up, from Punds Water, where you might have visited the two chambered cairns at the start of the walk.

Climb the opposite slope and look here for a ruined water-mill. Pass in front of a cottage, Pund of Mangaster, and walk on where spring squill grows in profusion. Now you go on over the short turf between the many rocky outcrops where wheatears flit and oyster-catchers pipe their warning calls.

Dawdle on past dwarf rose bushes clinging to the cliff face, and where tormentil spangles the heather and turf alike. Fulmars scold from the other side of a small bay, nesting on green ledges among a vast area of primroses and bird's-foot trefoil. Look for moss campion flowering among the ice-smoothed boulders, the colours of the little plant shading from white to deep mauve.

Cross the beck that flows into the bay, where butterwort thrives, and stroll on. Climb up above the bay and walk past a stone sheep pen. Walk along the headland and tread with care,

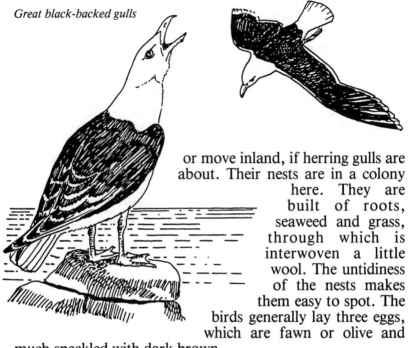

Great black-backed gulls

or move inland, if herring gulls are about. Their nests are in a colony here. They are built of roots, seaweed and grass, through which is interwoven a little wool. The untidiness of the nests makes them easy to spot. The birds generally lay three eggs, which are fawn or olive and much speckled with dark brown.

Walk with great care around the magnificent Black Skerry of Ramnageo, where roseroot grows in large masses. Seals haul out on the rocks far below. Cross a small burn that descends in a waterfall over the cliff. Continue over a glorious garden of flowers, then cross another burn, which falls over the cliff edge. Pass a sheep pen.

Then you come to a large flat area, with a stone cairn, and here great black-backed gulls glide. Oyster-catchers pipe loudly and mob the larger birds. Carry on around the headland to a much taller cairn. From here you have a wonderful view of the strange fangs of rocks called The Drongs, and of Dore Holm with its sea-chiselled arch.

Head on past a small lochan, where ringed plovers race across the sward. Ahead you can see St Magnus Hotel on Hillswick. Continue past Eina Stack and Mill Geos, where hundreds of fulmars nest around a huge natural arch. Head on along

Wilson's Noup, from where The Drongs seem very close and look like a Viking ship in full sail. From the next cairn you can glimpse the houses at Nibon and this is the way to walk.

Pass Moo Stack and then continue above South Sound, with the Isle of Nibon beyond. Descend the slope to pass a ruined crofthouse. Cross two burns and stroll on around the cliffs, now on the outside of the fence. Climb the next fence and walk on where spring squill grows out of the reach of sheep.

Descend the steepish slope to the side of the attractive shingle beach and walk towards the first house. Stroll on into this very bonny corner of North Mainland. Join the metalled road and follow it inland through a wild landscape of exposed rock, with barely a covering of soil. Higher up the slopes the forbidding heather moorland stretches away.

Stroll the quiet road, which runs above Gunnister Voe. Pass the deserted crofts of Gruna. Follow the road as it swings right to pass peat cuttings and an area where peat is being cut by machine. Here 'sausages' of peat, more than a hundred yards in length, lie in rows like dark brown corrugated paper. Stroll by Trolladale Water and on to join the A970 at Johnnie Mann's Loch. Cross the road and walk right to rejoin your car.

Three cairns

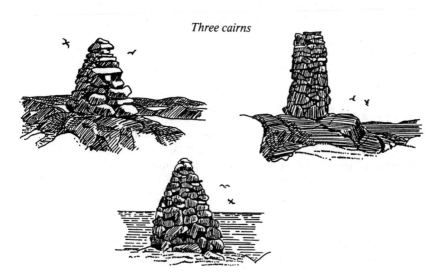

17. A Circular Walk from Hillswick

Information

Distance: 4½ miles
Time: 2-3 hours
Map: Landranger 3 Shetland, North Mainland
Terrain: Easy walking but walk with care.
Parking: 281766

A marvellous walk with something different to see round every corner.

The walk round the Ness of Hillswick is magnificent. It starts and ends gently, but towards the headland the cliffs are high, sheer and glorious. It is easy walking all the way but there are many dangerous edges, hidden until the last moment, so be wary — especially if walking with children. Dogs are not allowed.

The west branch of the A970 continues to the village of Hillswick. Drive along the narrow road to its end, where the farmer at Findlins has created a parking area near to the sturdy Findlins House. From here, walk back along the track and pass through a gate on your right, opposite The Smithy. Look for otters in the bay and for a colourful male red merganser idling on the water.

Go on along the shallow cliffs where, in spring, milkmaids and marsh marigolds thrive in a dampish area. Curlews,

wheatears, green plovers and oyster-catchers call from inland
pastures. Walk on over a carpet of silverweed and look for
turnstones feeding along the edge of the waves. Several black
guillemots bob gently on the water of Ura Firth.

At Tur Ness the sea has undermined the jagged rocks of the
cliff edge and created a clear pool through which you can see the
large many coloured cobbles on its bed. Spring squill, thrift,
kidney vetch and bird's-foot trefoil flower to the water's edge
and this is an idyllic corner. On the turf lousewort flowers,
partly parasitic on the roots of grass and heather.

Walk with care as the cliffs become higher and the path
steeper. Fulmars and kittiwakes nest on the ledges of the
natural rock gardens. Stroll on past a natural arch where
starlings are busy on the cliff face. Here the lovely roseroot
grows in profusion.

Continue along the way, where you might see old rabbit holes where an otter lies up. There are several entrances and outside are large piles of small pieces of shells of crustaceans and several spraints (droppings). Look for a low stack just offshore, quite white with scurvy grass.

Climb the fence and walk on through the territory of the skylark. Out to sea shags fly low. Pass a sheep pen where sea campion flowers. Then you come to a small stone ruin close to a burn. Here you may wish to make a detour by following the stream inland to see a ruined watermill. Continue along the stream to just before the Lochan of Niddister to see the remains of a prehistoric cairn or burial place. Walk left round the loch to a small promontory where there are stones from what was probably a burnt mound.

Roseroot

Return to the shore. At the Bight of Niddister concrete steps descend the shallow rocks from which boats set off with supplies for the lighthouse at Baa Taing. Begin the steady climb up the cliffs. Look for spectacularly layered rock formations that tilt vertically to the shore. As you stroll round the Queen Geos, where some of the rocks take on a diadem shape, you can see the settlement of Nibon (Walk 16) across the firth.

Follow the narrow path around the glorious headland, always prepared for it to end suddenly in a sheer drop. Here, the writer came across an otter that at first seemed to be asleep, but was, alas, dead. Follow the white and black posts, which lead you safely to the lighthouse on Baa Taing. From here, over St Magnus Bay, you can see the islands of Papa Stour and Foula, and Sandness Hill in West Mainland.

Go on around the headland, where buttercups flower among the spring squill and violets. From between Gordi Stack and Windy Geo you have a perfect view of the fantastically-shaped Drongs — weird-shaped pink granite stacks.

Cross the fence and then continue on to view the flower-topped Isle of Westerhouse from the Pund of Grevasand, where great care should be exercised.

Descend, and then climb to the highest point 82 metres (269 feet) of the cliffs. Descend again to Ber Dale, from where the wonderful red granite cliffs, the Heads of Grocken, welcome you. As you begin your approach to the village, a small flock of noisy grey-lag geese take off from feeding in the pasture. Keep to the outside of the fence and stroll the low cliffs to join a cart track. This continues to the left of a sturdy wall. Follow it round Sand Wick, close to a stretch of golden sand topped with pebbles. Follow a narrow path behind the beach that leads to another track. This runs along the far side of the oval-shaped walled cemetery, where once stood a medieval chapel. Look for the 18th-century headstones built into the wall on either side of the gate.

Walk into the village to pass the splendid white painted wooden St Magnus Hotel. Once it was owned by the North of Scotland, Orkney and Shetland Steam Navigation Company, who landed visitors here. It started life as a Norwegian pre-fabricated building in the 19th century, used for the Great Exhibition. Today it is privately owned and has a reputation for good food and hospitality.

Walk on to view St Magnus Church, built in 1870. Return past the hotel and turn left to see Shetland's oldest public house, The Booth (1698). At the time of writing it was closed for refurbishment. Head back towards the burial ground and continue along the narrow road to Findlins Farm, passing on the left a handsome large white house, The Manse. Walk on to rejoin your car.

18. A Circular Walk from Eshaness Lighthouse

Information

Distance: 4 miles
Time: 2-3 hours
Map: Landranger 3 Shetland, North Mainland
Terrain: Easy walking.
Parking: 205785

A good walk with lots of interest along the way.

To reach the lighthouse, drive through Mavis Grind, a thin strip of land with the North Sea on the right and the Atlantic on the left, and continue. Where the A970 divides, take the western (left) branch, in the direction of Urafirth. Look for the right turn, B9078, just before Hillswick and drive on to pass through Braewick. As you near the coast, follow the signpost for the lighthouse, which stands white and prominent on the cliffs ahead. There is ample parking and an information board.

Walk north (right) over the closely-cropped turf, colourful with low-growing thrift. Approach with care the edge of Calder's Geo, which is immensely deep, dark and extensive. You can see a cave far below, which is really a subterranean passage that links with the sea on the north side. The sides of the ravine support thrift, bird's-foot trefoil and spring squill, producing a wonderful natural rock garden. Here fulmars nest.

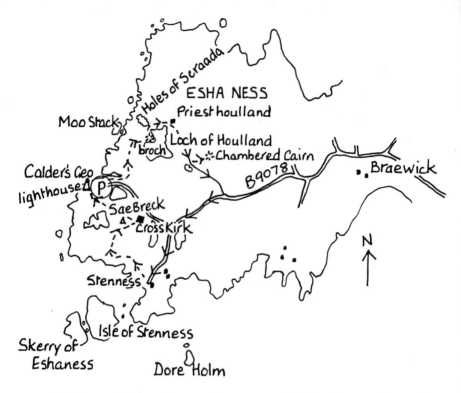

Walk north, keeping on the seaward side of several small
lochs, where thrift, spring squill and dark blue eyebright
flower. Climb the wall by a sturdy stile. Walk round another
huge geo and then go on to view the rugged Moo Stack, which is
lichen-covered and has a large natural arch. Climb a small slope
and look down on the tortured rocks of Scraada.

Return to the wall and continue down beside it to the Loch of
Houlland, on which stands a tall ruinous broch, dating from
the third century to the first century BC. Climb through the
outer wide-stone ramparts guarding access from the shore. Step
into the central hollow, where the walls are 12 feet high in parts.
In almost every crevice thrift now flowers.

Walk along the small stream that flows out of the loch.
It once powered several watermills, now also in ruins. Beyond,
is the dramatic blowhole known as the Hole of Scraada, where
the natural rock vault of subterranean caves has collapsed,

86

and into it the little burn tumbles. Be wary as you approach. The hole is very deep. It is connected to the sea by a tunnel, 110 yards long.

Walk round the end of the Loch of Houlland in a clockwise direction, heading towards a crofthouse, Priesthoulland. When level with the house, bear right along a wide grassy track to a gate. Beyond, turn right to walk a reinforced track that takes you through heather moorland — the territory of curlew, oyster-catcher, wheatear and arctic tern. Fom here you have a good view of Foula.

Stroll on until you are level with a lochan on your right. Then strike up left to the top of a small hill to see the March Cairn, a square-chambered cairn composed of large square boulders. It stands over four feet tall.

Return to the track and continue to the road. Turn right and walk ahead. To your far left look for The Drongs and, nearer, Dore Holm, with its huge natural arch through which a boat can pass.

Curlews

Dore Holm

Ignore the turn to the lighthouse and walk on to the end of the road at Stenness. The cross on the hill, overlooking the only working croft, was erected in 1927 by the Commissioners for Northern Lighthouses to mark the spot where supplies for the Eshaness lighthouse were landed. The settlement was once a fishing station. You can see the remains of five houses and a booth (where dealing or barter would have taken place) at the top of the fine pebble beach. Here, the open-sea fishermen would haul up their boats, and dry and salt their fish. The settlement was in an ideal situation because the returning boats and the station were sheltered by the Isle of Stenness and the Skerry of Eshaness. Today sheep are taken by boat onto the isle to graze.

Take the gate on the right at the end of the road and return along the shallow cliffs. Cross the fence and then walk up beside the wall to its end. Here you can see an old watermill. Pass through the gate and strike upwards towards the triangulation point on top of Sae Breck, from where you have a magnificent view. Look for traces of a broch. Sadly the triangulation point, a coastguard look-out and defence installations from the Second World War sit astride it.

Drop down the hill to visit the immaculately tended site of Cross Kirk, a medieval church. Here, in the middle of the cemetery, is the tomb of Donald Robertson, who died in 1848, aged 63. Legend tells that he was mistakenly given nitre instead of epsom salts and he died within five hours. Laurance Tulloch of Clothister, who made the mistake, rapidly left the district and set up shop in 1852 in Aberdeen. Johnny Notions (Walk 19) is also buried here.

Leave the cemetery and turn left to climb the slopes below Sae Breck. Follow the telegraph wires across the sward of spring squill and thrift towards the lighthouse and to rejoin your car.

19. A Circular Walk from Hamnavoe

Information

Distance: 4½ miles
Time: 2-3 hours
Map: Landranger 3 Shetland, North Mainland
Terrain: Easy walking. Can be wet in parts.
Parking: 243806

An interesting walk. The sudden approach towards the black cliffs is very exciting.

Drive the same route as for Walk 18. At Braewick, turn right, following the signpost directions for Hamnavoe. As you near the tiny settlement, look for the two large standing stones on the right of the single-track road. Park in the lay-by on the right, immediately beyond them, before the cattle grid.

Walk the mile-long track that leads off by the stones. This easy-to-walk way, reinforced in fine red stone, winds pleasingly through the heather of Grind Hill. Here nest curlew, oyster-catcher and wheatear. Continue past Mill Lochs and then Craagles Water. Pass through the gate in the sturdy wall. Ahead in the distance lies the crofthouse of Tingon, surrounded by green pastures.

Carry on until, well before the crofthouse, you reach the Burn of Tingon. It tumbles in pretty falls through masses of marsh marigold. To the right of the track stand the remnants

of a watermill and traces of its leat. Turn left before the tractor bridge and walk downstream, where many pairs of golden plovers call to each other.

Cross the fence and pass more attractive cascades. Look for a ruined crofthouse high on the slope on the opposite side of the

Standing stones

burn. Below stands a short, wide standing stone, leaning seawards. Continue on over a sward of thrift to pass through a gate in the fence. Carry on over an area of scattered boulders and old walls topped with lichen.

Then you reach a deep geo, named Warie Gill, where the Burn of Tingon descends in a long elegant waterfall. Here, the flaring cliffs are of great blocks of volcanic lava. Climb carefully to see two huge caves in the base of the great ravine. In every crevice of this black tumble of boulders flowers the ubiquitous thrift.

Turn left to walk back along the low hills known as the Villians of Hamnavoe. Spring turf edges the wide plates of lava, which stretch towards the sea. The turf is colourful with moss campion, spring squill, thrift and buttercup. Pass a small lochan and then continue to a cairn with pleasing views towards Eshaness. Far below a common seal stares from the water.

Climb, with care, the fencing at the shore end of a long wall. Here, fulmars nest towards the top of the geo. Head on, following a row of fence posts. These lead you across small streams, damp flushes where snipe feed, and on and on to another fence. Beyond head across, right, towards the boulder beach of Whal Wick. Climb the shallow cliff to go through a gate. Bear left across the pasture to pass a small lochan where arctic terns nest among the marsh marigolds on a small island. Continue to a gate to a track and follow this round to come to Johnny Notions' House, now a camping bod.

Johnny Notions, whose real name was John Williamson, was born in the middle of the 18th century. He developed a method of innoculation against smallpox, which had devastated Shetland throughout the 18th century. None of his patients ever became a victim.

Join the metalled road and walk down, and then uphill, to rejoin your car by the standing stones.

Common seals

20. A Circular Walk from North Roe, North Mainland

Information

Distance: 8-9 miles
Time: 4-5 hours
Map: Landranger 1 Shetland, Yell and Unst
Terrain: The track at the start is long and rough underfoot. The return over the cliffs is good roller-coaster hill walking.
Parking: 365898

This is a long and quite arduous walk and should be undertaken only by strong, well-equipped walkers. The rewards — the Neolithic axe factory, the island of Uyea and the return route along the coast to South Voe — make it an exciting trek.

Take the A970 into North Mainland. Drive below the red hills known as the Beorgs of Skelberry, where the bleakness makes you feel you have stepped into Iceland. Continue to the striking village of North Roe, passing first the school and then the church. Park opposite a small white wooden hut, used by the coastguard service.

Cross the road and follow the track that goes in front of the hut. Ignore the track that goes right, and stride on beside a dancing burn. The way makes for stark walking, as if the last glacier had only just passed through. Grey boulders lie scattered through the heather. At first, the only signs of life are the many green plovers, curlews, wheatears, oyster-catchers and arctic

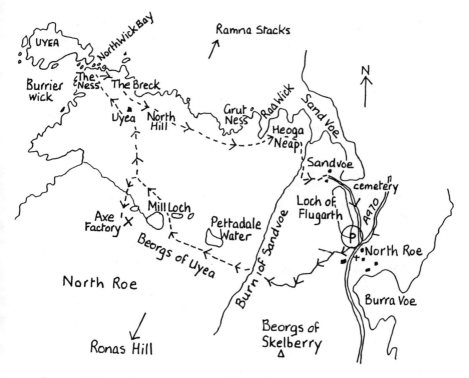

skuas. Then a human comes into view, cutting his peats and stacking them to dry — a traditional late spring job.

Keep to the main track as it swings right and pass through the first gate. Follow the wide track, a masterly piece of excavation through ten feet of peat in some places. It comes near to Pettadale Water and below the forbidding slopes of the Beorgs of Uyea. Then the gated way passes between Mill Loch and a lochan. Each time the way appears to branch, keep to the right fork until you can see the coast in the distance. Then you take a good left branch swinging up through the moorland towards the north-west end of the Beorgs of Uyea on your left. Climb to the fence coming in on your left.

Beyond, continue climbing through the heather and over a shattered mass of boulders to the cairn above. Walk east (diagonally left) a hundred yards above this to another cairn. Look for a smaller cairn, locating the Neolithic axe factory.

Neolithic axe factory

Here, in a hollow roofed with slabs, ancient man obtained pieces of speckled felsite rock, sharp enough to be used for cutting. Bracken and moss grow inside his factory now. Around the site lie piles of the unique blue stone, speckled as if hailstones had rained down, patterning the rock with symmetrical spots. Please do not take any samples from this magical site.

Return to the cairn and then drop downhill to the track. Turn right to return to the main track. Head left and stroll towards the crofthouse of Uyea, where the crofter is busy with lambing. What a glorious contrast from the moorland. The house is set in rolling greensward, and ewes and lambs seem everywhere, the air resounding with their bleating.

At the end of the track, walk on to The Ness and look across (depending on the tides) a spit of sand or the sea towards the grassy isle of Uyea, which is rich in copper. (People trying to cross the sand have been cut off by the tide — so be warned.) The grazing on the island is good and sheep are driven across the sand at low tide.

Turn east (right) to walk round North Wick Bay, where you pass the remains of several fishing huts. Follow the fence around The Breck and continue to join a good track. This leads you to the ruins of Brevligarth, with magnificent views as you go of Ramna Stacks, jutting skywards like jagged black teeth.

The cliffs, which receive the full force of the wind, are denuded of vegetation and the rock is weathered into tortured shapes. Stroll on, with care, around several very steep geos, colourful with cushions of moss campion, large clumps of

yellow roseroot
and patches
of pink thrift. Among
these nest many pairs
of fulmars, constantly
chattering to each other.

Climb North Hill, where
scattered patches of sandwort,
lichen and moss colonise the bare slopes and
summit. Where you descend the other side, wild
thyme grows. Cross a small burn bright with marsh marigolds.
In the next bay, several pairs of eiders swim close to large areas
of floating seaweed, making the ducks difficult to spot. Look
here for horizontal pink granite, intruding into grey vertical
layers of lava.

Continue over the close, short turf. Look out to sea, where
a flock of gannets continually dive for fish. Cross another
burn and pass by some small pools where common gulls
bathe. Clamber over an enormous boulder field that stretches
to the cliff edge of Grut Ness. Walk on round Raa Wick and
then, maintaining height, follow the contours round the
slopes to Heoga Neap. From here you can see Ronas Hill
and look back on the route you have walked. You also have
a good view of Fethaland and, with binoculars, your car at
North Roe.

Walk round the dramatic headland from which you have a
pleasing view of Sand Voe with its natural arches. A constant
stream of shags fly in and out of the inlet.

Then descend steadily to the tiny pebble shore far below, at
the foot of the Burn of Sandvoe. Walk inland, upstream,
passing the foundations of many a dwelling. Cross the end of a
track and walk on to a ruined watermill.

Return to the track and follow it uphill. Here, legend has it
that an 18th-century pirate was murdered by being buried alive
by his shipmates.

Continue along the track to pass a small loch, where a pair of red-throated divers idle and bogbean grows. Stroll on to the tiny hamlet of Sand Voe. Go on along the metalled road, with the lovely sandy bay of Sand Voe to your left and the Loch of Flugarth to your right. Pass the cemetery, where thrifts and primroses flower. Continue along the road to rejoin your car.

21. A Circular Walk on Fethaland

Information	
Distance:	6-7 miles
Time:	3-4 hours
Map:	Landranger 1 Shetland, Yell and Unst
Terrain:	Generally easy walking.
Parking:	372909

An exciting walk that should not be missed.

Fethaland, an unbelievably beautiful hilly place of green pastures and dramatic seascapes, is the most northerly point on Shetland's North Mainland. Take the A970 to Mavis Grind, a thin strip of land with the North Sea on the right and the Atlantic on the left, and then keep to the northern branch. Continue in the direction of North Roe, and then Isbister, where the road ends at a gate. A notice, 'Private Road', applies to cars; walkers have access. Dogs are prohibited. To the right, before the gate, is a parking lay-by.

Pass through the gate and follow the good track as it swings north, uphill. It is a breezy high-level way through sheep pasture, with occasional glimpses of sea and loch through the rolling hills. As you walk, remember the children who, as late as the early 1940s, trekked daily the almost trackless two miles, each way, between their homes and school.

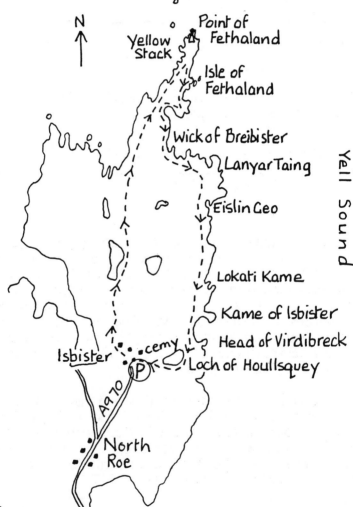

Ramna Stacks

Outer Booth

N

Point of Fethaland

Yellow Stack

Isle of Fethaland

Wick of Breibister

Lanyar Taing

Eislin Geo

Yell Sound

Lokati Kame

Kame of Isbister

Head of Virdibreck

Isbister   cemy

Loch of Houllsquey

P

A970

North Roe

Ruined fishing lodges at Fethaland

As you climb the hill, nothing prepares you for the magnificent view towards the Isle of Fethaland, a hilly, uptilting green headland that leans dramatically towards you — and hides even more glory beyond.

Below you, the isle is linked with Fethaland by a wonderful spit of boulders and pebbles a tenth of a mile in width, approached by a greensward covered with thrift. It separates the Atlantic from Yell Sound and on a glorious summer's day, with the wind in the right direction, the rollers come crashing in one side while gentle turquoise waves lap the other. To the left of the spit, a huge embankment of great boulders, ten feet high, has been thrown up. Below it grey seals bob.

On the spit stand a dozen or more ruined fishing lodges, once used by deep-sea fishermen between early June and the middle of August. Today these roofless, heavily-lichened, picturesque dwellings belie the noise and bustle of a once-busy station. Only the waves, the oyster-catchers and the fulmars break the silence.

Continue over the boulder spit and, on the island, pass through a gap in a ruined wall and ascend the grassy path ahead. Walk with care along the sheer west cliffs to see the jagged Yellow Stack close to the squat white lighthouse. Beyond, the high land narrows and drops to The Point of Fethaland, where spring squill covers the grass like blue snow.

Pause here and look out to see the lighthouse, with the massive Ramna Stacks (an RSPB reserve) beyond.

Turn south and walk back along the east coast of the isle to pass several geos, including Cleber Geo. Here, look for a large rock face of soapstone, once much quarried for bowls and pots. It is heavily carved with ancient graffiti.

Cross the spit and begin your return, left, along the east coast of the delightful promontory. Pass round the wide Wick of Breibister, below a ruined croft and watermill. Dawdle across Lanyar Taing and then on to pass an old sheep enclosure. On the slopes above, a huge rock of quartz catches the sunlight. Walk with care the edge of the very deep Eislin Geo, where primroses, roseroot and kidney vetch give it a golden glow. Innumerable fulmars and some kittiwakes brood their young, and shags fly into and out of their untidy nests far below.

Climb the next two fences and continue over the flower-spangled pasture, past another great sea bight into this riven eastern face. Approach circumspectly an overhanging crag, split down the middle, with a cave below.

Shags

Negotiate the third fence and then drop down to cross a hollow, through which runs a small burn and where considerable drainage work has been done. Pass the remains of more sheep enclosures. Just beyond, and before the next fence, look left and out onto Lokati Kame, the flat top of which appears to be a stack. In fact it is joined, at its base, by a knife-edge of rock. Here, you can see, from afar (do not cross the knife-edge), the grass-covered oblong-shaped foundations of a possible Celtic monastic site. You can just discern two compartments, with an entrance on the seaward side. In Walk 22 a similar site is seen, on the Birrier on Yell. Below this ancient site is a splendid natural arch.

Cross the next fence and stride on to walk, warily, round two huge grassy hollows that slope down to small stony beaches. Overlooking the second is the towering Head of Virdibreck. Climb to the top to see another monastic site. Look northward across the beach far below to a rocky promontory topped by a greensward that slopes towards the sea and is therefore visible only from the top of the Head. The promontory is known as the Kame of Isbister. On the greensward you can see the grassy outlines of the walls of four or five buildings.

Return to the foot of the hill and bear left to walk beside the Loch of Houllsquey, where a pair of red-throated divers idle on the glass-like water. Cross the fence, on your right, at the end of the loch and walk the south shore to join a good track. Follow this as it steadily descends towards Isbister, keeping below the slopes on your right. Here, a pair of snipe drum as they whirl like miniature planes high above. Pass between two dwellings surrounded by a vast area of wild irises.

Visit the cemetery of St Magnus, which has interesting 'gravestones' made of wood. Continue along the track to a gate, and turn left to rejoin your car.

22. A Circular Walk from West Sandwick, Island of Yell

Information

Distance: 7 miles
Time: 3-4 hours
Map: Landranger 1 Shetland, Yell and Unst
Terrain: Easy walking most of the way. Could be wet between the two lochs.
Parking: 454895

An interesting walk with grand views.

The roll-on roll-off ferry leaves Toft on the north-east coast of Mainland for Ulsta, South Yell, almost every half-hour throughout the day. The crossing takes approximately 20 minutes and the cost of travel is very reasonable. There are the usual concessions. Advance booking is essential. The inter-island ferries booking office telephone number is 01957 722259 or 722268.

Leave the pier at Ulsta by the A968 and drive for six miles to take the third turn on the left. Descend for a tenth of a mile and park on a lay-by at the side of the turn for Harkland.

Stride on down the road to West Sandwick, with the Loch of Scattlands to your left. Look for marsh marigolds, milkmaids and bird's-foot trefoil in the ditch at the side of the road. Elder and rose bushes thrive in cottage gardens, and bluebells flower along the roadside.

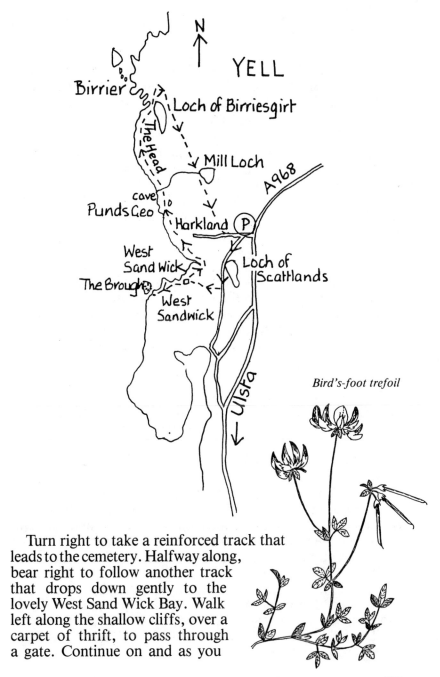

N

YELL

Birrier

Loch of Birriesgirt

The Head

Mill Loch

A968

cave

Punds Geo

Harkland ⓟ

West
Sand Wick

Loch of
Scattlands

The Brough

West
Sandwick

Ulsta

Bird's-foot trefoil

Turn right to take a reinforced track that leads to the cemetery. Halfway along, bear right to follow another track that drops down gently to the lovely West Sand Wick Bay. Walk left along the shallow cliffs, over a carpet of thrift, to pass through a gate. Continue on and as you go look for a low natural arch where the deep blue water of the sea turns to green.

Cross a tiny pebble beach — difficult perhaps when there is an exceptionally high tide. Then scramble up the stepped gneiss rock face to the broch, which has an outer rampart on the north side. What a glorious look-out!

Return to the sandy beach, where marram grass clothes the sand dunes. Here, the youngest walkers may like to enjoy the glorious rock pools and the sand. Then step across the narrow burn that flows out of the loch seen earlier. Ascend the shallow cliff and carry on north, along the seaward side of the fence.

From now on the walk has all the ingredients to make it superb. Look for thrift, moss campion, bird's-foot trefoil, butterwort and spring squill, growing in profusion. Grey seals laze on the rocks and others peer as you pass. Overhead fly curlew, whimbrel, wheatear, shag, raven, green plover, twite and oyster-catcher. The plaintive call of golden plover and the delightful trilling of dunlin carry far over the pastures.

Continue round Punds Geo, where the schist is laid in vertical sheets. Clamber down carefully to the entrance to a large cave, where moss campion flowers in the crevices. Return to the cliff top and cross the burn that flows out of Mill Loch and look upstream to see a ruined watermill.

Ascend The Head, crossing two fences. At the top, you have a first view of the Loch of Birriesgirt. Descend gently to the side of the burn that leaves the loch and tumbles in three graceful falls before reaching the sea. Stroll round the landward side of the fence and begin the ascent of the dramatic Birrier. Continue until you can see the oddly-shaped pinnacle of rock, aptly named The Old Wife of Birrier. Beyond the pinnacle, on the flat-topped continuation of the jutting promontory, it is thought that there might have been a monastic settlement, similar to that seen on the Kame of Isbister (Walk 21) which it faces across Yell Sound.

Now start your return. Strike inland for 50 yards and descend towards the Loch of Birriesgirt, seen earlier. On the way, look for a circle of rocks in the grass, with a scattering of stones of various sizes. This is believed to be a burnt mound.

Continue to the pleasing loch, where dunlin race along its sandy shore and wade in the shallows, catching prey. Stroll on along the east side of the quiet sheet of water. Keep on in the same direction past the loch, steadily ascending left over heather moorland with much peat. Look back for a grand view of the Birrier and its Old Wife.

As you breast a small rise, look ahead to see the track striding through the heather to the skyline. You should aim to join it just above Mill Loch, from which issues the burn that produces the waterfalls. Stride on along the track, ignoring two that lead off right, and continue for nearly three-quarters of a mile. Follow it as it bears left to join the road, up which you walk to rejoin your car.

West Sand Wick Beach

23. A Circular Walk from Gloup, Island of Yell

Information

Distance: 2 miles
Time: 2 hours
Map: Landranger 1 Shetland, Yell and Unst
Terrain: Easy walking over the tops. Take care along the side of the voe.
Parking: 506046

A short evening stroll with wonderful views.

Gloup was the second largest fishing station in Shetland when open boats with square sails, crewed by six men, were in use. It lies to the north of Yell and is reached by the A968, B9082, B9083, and then a narrow road. Park in a lay-by just beyond the signpost to the fishermen's memorial.

Walk the reinforced track to see the moving memorial to the 58 fishermen who perished when a great storm arose while they were deep-sea fishing in July 1881. The names of the boats and the crew, and where they lived, are listed on the memorial. Above the list is a carved statue of a woman and child, the woman with her hand shading her eyes as she peers out to sea. The woman and child represent the many widows and father-less children left after the tragedy. The memorial was erected in 1981.

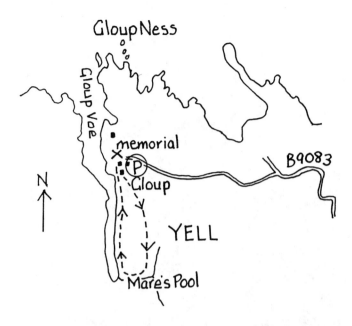

Climb the fence and walk on along the side of the dramatic voe. Beyond the gate in the next fence, climb steadily left to join a track. When the track swings into the hills, walk right across the rough pasture. You have a bird's-eye view of the inlet deep in its ravine of gneiss and of the wild moorland around.

Walk the high level way, with curlews, wheatears, twites, arctic and great skuas and a pair of merlins for company, until you come level with the Mare's Pool, below, at the head of the voe. Here, you may wish to descend almost to the shore and return along a narrow path just above the water. Or you may prefer to return by the same route for a glorious view of the coast, which gets better with every step you take.

Merlins

109

Fishermen's memorial, Gloup

24. A Circular Walk from Breakon, Island of Yell

Information

Distance: 3 miles
Time: 2 hours
Map: Landranger 1 Shetland, Yell and Unst
Terrain: Easy walking all the way.
Parking: 529045

A pleasing short walk along sandy bays and over dramatic cliffs.

To reach Breakon, drive in the same direction as for Walk 23 and park two miles before Gloup in a large lay-by close to the signpost for the Sands of Breakon. Walk down the side turn to pass a striking white house, with red doors and window frames, which is thought to date from the middle of the 18th century. Continue to the end of the road and the farm of Breakon. A signpost directs you right, across a gated pasture, and says that dogs are allowed by arrangement.

Follow the path to cross a stream, where in spring a mass of marsh marigolds grows. Pass through the gate and carry on. Now marram grass binds the sand on both sides. To your left lies the glorious shell-sand beach where, if the weather is good, you could linger a long time.

You may wish to walk the long grassy headland, which shelters the Wick of Breakon from the north-easterly winds, or you can cut across the end and walk on, with great care, as

YELL

N

Cullivoe

you approach the dramatic cliffs of the Ness of Houlland. Here, fulmars, kittiwakes and ravens nest. Then continue round the spectacular Brei Wick, with a grand view across to Unst.

Head on until you come to Kirk Loch. Cross the exit stream close to the lovely sandy stretch of water and continue right,

Remains of St Olaf's, Kirk of Ness

to a gate into the cemetery. In the centre stands all that remains of the church of St Olaf, Kirk of Ness, which served North Yell until the middle of the 18th century. Wander around the grave-stones and read the personal tragedies inscribed on some of them. A sturdy wall encloses the graveyard.

Return around the loch and climb the slope. Descend the other side and continue across the pastures to the prominent broch, dating between 100 BC and 200 AD, on the cliff edge. All that remains are the low inner walls and traces of two earth banks that once encircled it. Below is a later square dry-stone building known as a skeo; the wind blew through the gaps and dried meat and fish hanging inside. Inland, look for mounds of stones, known as clearance cairns.

Walk on along the west side of the Bay of Brough. Pass through a gate and continue along the beach. Here, on rocks in the bay, many seals haul out, others come very near the shore and watch. Look for sanderling, ringed plover and turnstones busy along the shoreline. From here there is a magnificent view across Bluemull Sound, where the deep blue sea turns to cream as it licks against the stacks, jagged boulders and skerries.

Shetland ponies

Head on across a shingle spit where silverweed grows. Keep to the seaward side of the Loch of Papil to join a track running inland, where Shetland ponies graze. The track leads to Duncan Fraser's well stocked shop. Carry on where the track becomes metalled to pass Cullivoe Primary School. At the T-junction, turn right and stride the narrow road between sheep pastures. At the branching of the road, bear left and walk on. Pass the pleasingly restored Haa of Houlland, a fine house built around the mid-18th century.

Stride the road to rejoin your car.

25. A Walk from Gutcher on the Island of Yell

Information

Distance: 5½ miles
Time: 3 hours — or more if otter-watching
Map: Landranger 1 Shetland, Yell and Unst
Terrain: Easy walking all the way.
Parking: 549993

This is THE otter walk. Approach quietly, sit and watch, either early in the day or late in the evening, and you will generally be rewarded.

This walk starts at Gutcher, North Yell. To reach the village, follow the instructions for Walk 22 and then follow the signs for the Gutcher ferry. Park near the pier, where there is a cafe, and good facilities. Walk towards the pier and climb the fence on the right to walk south, just outside the fence. Pass a crofthouse and then a house. Just beyond is a mound of stones, once the site of a medieval chapel.

To the left lies Linga. Continue past a ruined crofthouse to climb the fence beyond. Walk right to see a standing stone, about five feet tall, heavily encrusted with lichen.

Stride over the pastures of the shallow cliffs, which resound to the songs of skylarks. Wheatears flit about the tufts of grass and great and arctic skuas sail overhead and perch on a high point of herbage and watch. Seals peer out of the waves.

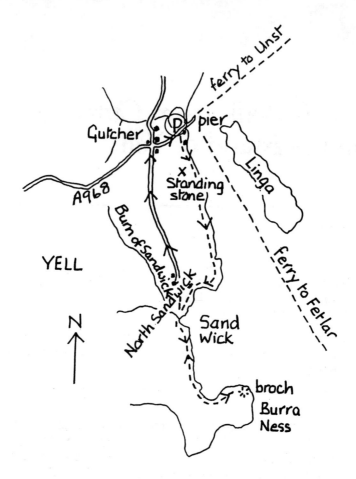

Stroll on along the low cliffs, taking care as you begin the descent to Sand Wick Bay. This area is well-known for otters. Approach quietly. Watch for a small head above the water. If you see an otter and it has a fish, it may lie on its back to deal with it. Then it will dive, its body and then its tail following the head with perfect co-ordination of movement. Seeing your first otter is a magical moment.

Pass a ruined crofthouse and go on round the bay. Look for clumps of thrift, thriving where it is out of reach of the hungry sheep. A pair of red mergansers swim just offshore. Cross the shingle spit, which has lovely sand to the seaward side. Step across the narrow Burn of Sandwick. Look here for a handsome turnstone lingering on its way to other lands — it is not known to nest in Great Britain. On the northern shore of the bay are two nousts into which boats were drawn.

Ahead lies the Burra Ness Broch, proudly overlooking the sound to the island of Fetlar. It stands quite 12 feet high on the seaward side and its wall is very thick. All around the grass is bright green, evidence that the land was under cultivation for a long time.

Otter

Return round Sand Wick Bay and cross the small burn. Look for a gate in the fence and pass through. Continue uphill in the

Burra Ness Broch

direction of the chimmey pots of North Sandwick, which you can just glimpse. Ascend the pastures, making sure to shut all the gates, to come to the start of the metalled road. Walk the narrow road as it crosses the moorland. Soon Gutcher comes into view. Its two colourful ferries, from Unst and Fetlar, approach or leave the pier. At the crossroads, turn right to descend the hill to rejoin your car.

26. A Circular Walk from Hamnavoe, Island of Yell

Information

Distance: 4½ miles
Time: 2-3 hours
Map: Landranger 2 Shetland, Whalsay
Terrain: Easy walking most of the way, but find the easiest way across the hummocks of heather.
Parking: 494804

A pleasing walk in a quiet corner of Yell.

To reach the Island of Yell, follow the instructions at the start of Walk 22. Leave the ferry at Ulsta and take the B9081, signposted to Burravoe. Park close to the parish church of Yell, St Magnus, a fine white building built in the early 19th century.

Leave the B-road and walk up the side turn, signposted Hamnavoe. On either side, in spring, grow marsh marigolds and flags and you can see many pairs of golden plovers. Follow the road left and then walk on to cross a cattle grid and a bridge over a tributary of the Burn of Hamnavoe. Stride on until just before the buildings at the road end. Strike right, at the easiest point of access, and keep to the same contour round Beaw Field, so avoiding the forbidding peat hags on the low summit. Follow sheep trods until you are above the small loch, named Evra Water.

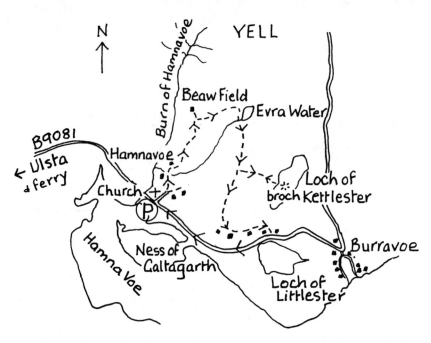

Drop down the slope and cross more peat to walk round the southern end of the sheet of water. Here, you might see red-throated divers, arctic and great skuas and whimbrel. Join the second, higher, of two tracks that lead off south (right) from the loch and begin your return.

Church of St Magnus

The good track passes through vast areas of heather moorland, a glorious sight in August/September, and the haunt of dunlin, oyster-catchers and common gull. Continue to the first plantiecrub and head left across the heather, if you wish, to see a broch, approached by a 50-foot stone causeway, towards the southern end of Loch Kettlester. In the bushes that thrive in the broch a blackbird nests.

Return to the good track and continue ahead, passing through a row of plantiecrubs. Stride on, with extensive views ahead. Look for the islands of Out Skerries and Whalsay, and then follow the track until you come to a fenced quarry. Continue left round the outside of the fence until you reach the access track to the quarry. Follow this to join the B-road close to the Loch of Littlester. Turn right and walk along the narrow road, with pleasing views of the Ness of Galtagarth, to rejoin your car.

27. A Circular Walk from Loch of Snarravoe, Island of Unst

Information

Distance: 6 miles
Time: 3-4 hours
Map: Landranger 1 Shetland, Yell and Unst
Terrain: Easy walking all the way.
Parking: 574017

A walk full of evidence of Shetland's ancient past.

Unst is Shetland's most northerly island and the third largest. It is reached by a car and passenger ferry from Gutcher on the Island of Yell. The crossing takes about 10 minutes and the boats run most efficiently, every half-hour, every day. The fare is very inexpensive. It is also possible to fly to the island, landing at Baltasound.

Drive along the A968 from the ferry for just under a mile. Park in a convenient lay-by beside the road, when the head of Loch of Snarravoe comes into view.

Take the track that drops steadily down, north (left), and follow it around the head of the loch. To your right, look for a small ruined watermill where a pretty crop of flags grows in the stream that powered the water wheel. Note that this is the point to which you return at the end of the walk.

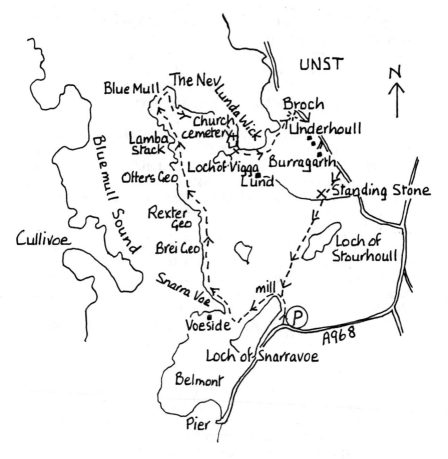

Continue above the shore, where butterwort and milkmaids flower. Pass below a small ruined settlement and then bear right, crossing a wet area where snipe feed, to the edge of Snarra Voe. From here, there is a pleasing view of Cullivoe, and its white painted Church of St Olaf, on the Island of Yell, across the Bluemull Sound.

To the left of the bay lies the ruined Voeside, where once the ferry from Cullivoe docked. Walk right along the pebbly beach. Look for the dark-coloured Shetland wrens courting about the boulders. Continue on the shallow cliffs to pass a noust and the end of an ancient wall. At Brei Geo, fulmars have taken up residence on the many grassy flats of the cliff face.

Carry on along the lovely way, over vast flowerings of thrift. Skylarks, wheatears, oyster-catchers, curlews and great skuas are all to be seen. Climb the fence. Look for the pale mauve flowers of the butterwort in the wet flushes. Now you can see the northern end of Yell and the calmer waters of the sound change to a heavy swell as you near the open sea.

Walk circumspectly round Rexter Geo, where there are great clumps of moss campion and thrift. Here, the sea turns to a rich green as it passes below a large natural arch. From caves come the eerie calls of nesting shags. Look down the steep cliffs to see a small group of black guillemots, their red legs, like paddles, splayed out as they duck below the surface.

Head on to Otters Geo, where more shags nest. Stand with care overlooking Lamba Stack to view more caves and two magnificent arches in the geo. Dawdle past a wall on your right and then begin the gentle climb up the grassy slopes of Blue Mull. Follow the good path to the top and then descend gently to a wide grassy flat, defended by rocks, with a dramatic view over Lunda Wick and along the north west coast of the island.

Bear right, round The Nev, to come to the remains of a small, possibly ancient, watch tower. Walk on well above the shore to pass the other end of the wall passed on your approach to Blue Mull. Look ahead to the skyline, over the Loch of Vigga, to see the gaunt ruins of the 18th-century Lund Hall.

Cross below another extensive wall and walk the short turf. Look carefully into small geos where primroses flower from cliff top to water's edge. Continue to the ruined church of St Olaf's — the gate is on the far wall of the cemetery. Go through the entrance of the little church and walk to the end. Look up under the lintel of the tiny window on your right to see a carving of a fish. Close by the lintel is a badly-eroded tombstone. It marks the place where a 16th-century Bremen merchant, Segebad Detken, was buried. Details of the inscription, now gone, are to be found in the Pier House Museum (a restored Hanseatic bod) at Symbister on Whalsay (Walk 37).

Look in the churchyard for another gravestone of a Bremen merchant, for several small stone crosses and for the headstone of Peter Harper, which carries a quaint legend. Bluebells, red campion and milkmaids flower close to lichened walls.

Memorial stone

IN MEMORY OF
PETER BRUCE HARPER
SON OF ALEXR JAS HARPER
& WILLIAMINA JOHNSTON
WHO DIED 8TH JANY
1854
WEEP NOT FOR ME, MY PARENTS DEAR
I AM NOT DEAD, BUT SLEEPING HERE
MY CLASS IS RUN, MY GRAVE YOU SEE
SHURE, PREPARE TO FOLLOW ME.
TIME FLYS!

Walk across the glorious sands of Lunda Wick, where arctic terns capture sand eels. Climb up the pebbles at the far end, and step across a little stream to a gate through the fence. Head straight up, with the fence to your right, to another gate. Beyond, bear left to cross a wet area. Continue over another fence and keep walking left until you reach Underhoull, the site of a Norse settlement. Excavation in the 1960s revealed a longhouse with a small area for animals at the south end. Notice the long passage to the house.

Climb straight up the hill and cross the stile into the remains of the broch of Underhoull. The Vikings removed the broch's stone to build their dwelling. The broch was defended by a double rampart and two quite deep 'moats', bridged by a causeway. From the broch continue ahead to the fence and then walk right to a gate to the road.

Turn right and stroll along the quiet way. Ignore the turn to Burragarth and continue to a cattle grid. Look right to see a tall standing stone of gneiss. Pass

Bluebell

through the gate on the right and head across the heather moorland to the narrow road, leading to the stone. Look for golden plover and snipe.

Cross the road and climb the track, which leads to a gate on the skyline. To your left lies the Loch of Stourhoull, where more red-throated divers swim. Beyond the gate, turn left to pass through another. Turn right to continue uphill and walk to the right of a ruined crofthouse. On a large wet area to your right a pair of teal swim.

Walk on, descending steadily, left, below another ruined crofthouse. Aim for the little watermill seen at the beginning of the walk. Beyond stretches the Loch of Snarravoe. Join the track and walk uphill to rejoin your car.

28. A Circular Walk from The Ness, Burra Firth, Island of Unst

---

Information

Distance: 6 miles
Time: 3-4 hours
Map: Landranger 1 Shetland, Yell and Unst
Terrain: Easy walking all the way.
Parking: 612149

This long, challenging walk is every ornithologist's dream.

To get to Unst, follow the instructions given for Walk 27. To reach the Scottish Natural Heritage reserve at the north end of the island, leave the ferry by the only road, the A968, and continue. Near Haroldswick, look for the signpost directing you left to Burrafirth. Almost at the end of the road, the right branch leads to a large building that was once the shore station for the Muckle Flugga lighthouse. The warden of the reserve, who lives here, welcomes visitors and is very helpful.

The left branch of the road leads to a car park for the reserve, where there is an information board. Pass through the two kissing-gates and follow the clear track through the heather. Soon waymarker posts, topped with green paint, guide you on your way.

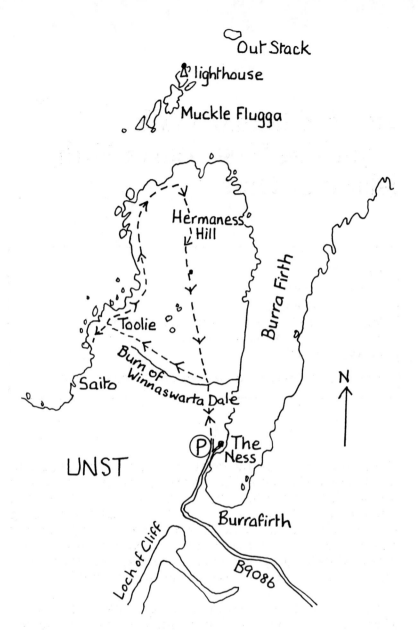

Out Stack

lighthouse

Muckle Flugga

Hermaness
Hill

Burra Firth

Toolie

Saito

Burn of
Winnaswarta Dale

N

UNST

P The
Ness

Burrafirth

Loch of Cliff

B9086

At the Burn of Winnaswarta Dale, the track bears left through a sheltered hollow, where croziers of bracken are appearing. Just beyond the hollow, the path climbs a slope and the way divides. Walk ahead, following the posts beside the burn. Ignore those up the slope on the right — that is the way to return.

Gannets

The marker posts take you safely, west, across the peaty moorland. Here, you pass through the territories of golden plover, wheatear, skylark, oyster-catcher and great skua. You are asked to keep to the path to avoid erosion and not to disturb this unique area of nesting birds.

Nothing prepares you for what awaits as you near the very high cliffs — first the noise, then the smell, and finally the sight of thousands of gannets nesting on the sheer cliffs, the latter a brilliant white from the guano. Walk left along the precipitous cliffs to see the ledges lined with birds. The nests are made of turf or seaweed and lined with all sorts of oddments. A pair of sunglasses was found in one gannet's nest.

Across a small bay at Saito, sitting alone but close to the gannets, is an albatross, named Albert by the people of Unst. It was believed to be five years old when it arrived, ten years ago, and has been returning each year since. Sometimes it thinks it is a fulmar and tries to mate with one. It is difficult to spot, living as it does with the large white gannets.

Walk on in the same direction, watching for puffins as they glide in with red legs splayed. They land close to their burrows and then disappear into them. Further round the cliffs, where there are even more gannets, look far down to a wide ledge, white with guano, to see rows of guillemots, all facing into the cliff. Fulmars nest on any grassy ledge, among the thrift. Here and there a few kittiwakes reside. Through all these birds, pairs of great skuas dive, looking for suitable victims.

Return back along the cliff to the last marker post. Ignore the track, right, and continue north along the cliffs. Drop down the slope to cross a small stream. Look inland to see a sheep pen where you might decide to picnic if the wind is strong.

Walk on along the coast to perhaps even more spectacular sitings of gannets. Here, too, the pinnacles of rock are completely white. Look down onto ledges far below where more guillemots nest and shags use the few remaining sites. Here, the cliffs are pocked with puffin burrows and the comical-looking birds continually come and go.

Then you can see the sturdy, seemingly stumpy, lighthouse on Muckle Flugga, beloved by photographers, who carry their tripods over the peaty tops. Beyond lies Out Stack, the most northerly point of Great Britain.

When you can bear to leave this glorious coastline, follow the green-topped posts up Hermaness Hill and then descend over the heather moorland. Do not stray from the path into the very boggy environs. Continue past the remains of a hut, blown away in a gale. Look right to see a small lochan where three dozen great skuas gather. Use the duckboards over the peat hags and be grateful to the volunteers who have made the walk so much more pleasant.

On joining the outward path by the burn, bear left and follow the waymarked route to rejoin your car.

Hermaness Hill

29. A Circular Walk to the Horse Mill of Hagdale and the Keen of Hamar, Island of Unst

Information

Distance: 1½ miles
Time: 1 hour
Map: Landranger 1 Shetland, Yell and Unst
Terrain: Easy walking.
Parking: 636098

A short walk but a botanist's dream.

To reach the mill, and the low hill known as the Keen of Hamar, leave the ferry terminal on Unst as for Walk 27. Drive along the A968 to the north side of Baltasound. Look for the signpost, directing you right, for the Horse Mill of Hagdale. Park near the start of the track to the mill.

Pass through a kissing-gate to walk along the track through disused workings. Here, chromate of iron, used in explosives and for metal plating, was quarried until 1944. Follow the track to the end, where stands the partially-restored circular stone mill. Horses, treading the paved way at the base of the wall, turned the large stones, still present, to grind the chromate ore. A small stream runs into the stone socket onto the revolving stones.

Leave the mill and walk across the pasture towards a stile in the fence, which gives access to the foot of Hamar — hamar

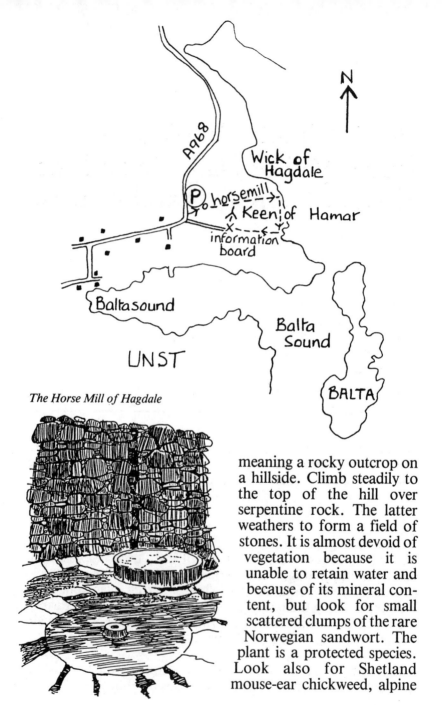

The map shows:

N ↑

A968

Wick of Hagdale

P to horsemill →

Keen of Hamar

information board

Baltasound

Balta Sound

UNST

BALTA

The Horse Mill of Hagdale

meaning a rocky outcrop on a hillside. Climb steadily to the top of the hill over serpentine rock. The latter weathers to form a field of stones. It is almost devoid of vegetation because it is unable to retain water and because of its mineral content, but look for small scattered clumps of the rare Norwegian sandwort. The plant is a protected species. Look also for Shetland mouse-ear chickweed, alpine scurvy grass, moss campion, thrift, clubmoss and the northern fen orchid.

Climb to the top over this stark stone field, which looks the way much of Britain probably looked at the end of the Ice Age. Walk right to the fence. Do not cross, but walk right, downhill, with the fence to your left. At the corner, turn right again and continue downhill. At the fence corner, pass through the gate to read the information board, which has been provided by the National Nature Reserve. Return through the gate and walk beside the fence, now on your left. Continue until you reach the stile you crossed at the start of your ascent of the Keen. Stride across the pasture to the horse mill and return along the track to the kissing-gate to rejoin your car.

Shetland mouse-ear chickweed

30. A Circular Walk from Muness Castle, Island of Unst

Information

Distance: 4½ miles
Time: 2 hours
Map: Landranger 1 Shetland, Yell and Unst
Terrain: Easy walking all the way.
Parking: 629011

A delight to walk.

To reach Unst, follow the instructions for Walk 27. Leave the ferry by the A968, the only road, and take the first right turn, the B9084, signposted Muness Castle. Continue through the picturesque Uyeasound, once a busy herring port, past Easter Loch via a causeway, and on through Clivocast. Look for a standing stone close to the road on the right, with Skuda Sound beyond. Ignore all right turns until you reach the castle. Park tidily close by. The key, a torch and a leaflet are obtained from a white cottage just over a green.

Muness Castle

The castle was built in 1592 by Laurence Bruce, half-brother to Robert Stewart, illegitimate son of James V, and was inhabited until 1699. It is

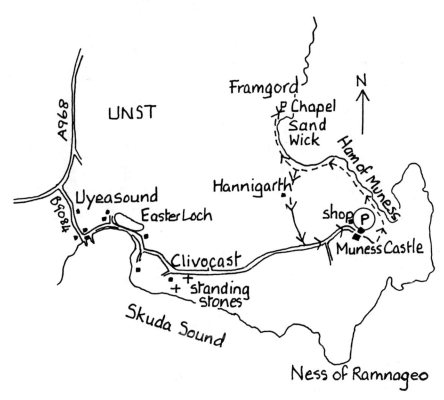

oblong-shaped and has step gabling and round towers. It has been partially restored and is a magical place to wander. Each chamber has been labelled and there is an information panel by the entrance.

Continue down the metalled road towards the shore. Bear left across to the Ham of Muness, using gates, and crossing fences with care. Walk left in the direction of Sand Wick Bay. Keep along the shallow cliffs, which are frequently indented by geos. Fulmars nest on the ledges. Thrift grows along the way. Overhead fly great skuas, hoodies, ravens, oyster-catchers and curlews.

Continue past a ruined medieval building, which looks rather like a miniature castle. Out to sea common seals peer. Carry on to take the stile to the large, lovely white-sand bay. Here, great deep blue rollers change to turquoise, topped with surf, as they come roaring in. You will wish to linger.

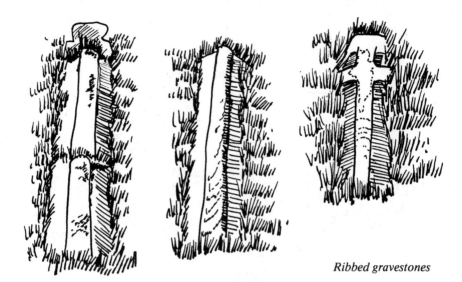

Ribbed gravestones

Cross the sands, over silver weed and thistles, to a gate at the far end of the bay. Head on above the shore towards a sturdy walled enclosure. On the far side is the entrance to the little chapel and burial ground of Framgord. Wander at will through this peaceful corner. Look for the ribbed gravestones and ancient stone crosses. Here grow blue, white and pink bluebells. Many headstones make sad reading. Above the church stand ruined crofthouses.

Return to the bay and walk the wind-rippled sand, beside the fence on your right. Here, great sand mounds covered with glasswort project eerily. At the end of the fence, turn inland to walk beside another. Continue to the corner of two fences. Turn left and keep to the left of the cottage, Hannigarth, to a stile to an access track. Walk ahead to a stile onto a metalled road, which you cross. Pass through a gate opposite — it has two strong bolts — and walk the continuing track. The gated way is easy to follow and climbs steadily through heather moorland, where curlews and green and golden plovers nest.

Stride to the road and walk left. The castle soon comes into view. Before you rejoin your car, visit the shop run by Margaret Peterson, where you can view spinning and weaving. She also has a small cafe and makes a very good cup of tea.

31. A Circular Walk on the Island of Fetlar

Information

Distance: 3½ miles
Time: 2 hours or more, depending on the time spent in the bird hide
Map: Landranger 1 Shetland, Yell and Unst
Terrain: Easy walking all the way.
Parking: 656900

A delightful walk. Leave yourself time to use the bird hide.

Fetlar lies south of the Island of Unst and measures about five miles by two-and-a-half miles. It is a green island with very little peat. The grass provides rich grazing for many sheep. The northern part of the island is heath, which supports a wealth of plant life and birds.

A ferry from Gutcher, on the Island of Yell, takes you to Oddsta, Fetlar. It is not as frequent as those to Unst, so consult your timetable and book in advance (telephone 01957 722259 or 722268). The journey, which is inexpensive, takes 25 minutes.

Leave the pier by the only road and drive along the B9088 almost to the end of the road. Look for the RSPB notice board by Funzie (pronounced Finnie) Loch and park close by. Follow the blue waymarks to pass the Loch of Funzie. Here,

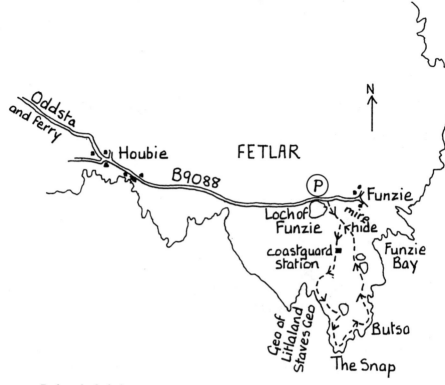

Red-necked phalaropes

red-throated divers and rare red-necked phalaropes breed and you are asked not to walk around the loch to avoid disturbing them.

Continue to the bird hide, opened in 1989, and look out over the mire of Funzie. Until 1973, the phalaropes bred in this wet area regularly. Then the area became drier and they ceased to breed. Since 1986, the RSPB has managed the marsh by creating small pools, maintaining a higher water level and reintroducing controlled grazing. In late spring, the mire is a blaze of golden marsh marigolds that are followed by flags and cotton grass. Look for snipe, dunlin and ringed plover. Otters too are seen occasionally.

Return to the loch and take the wide grassy track that climbs through the heather to the disused coastguard look-out station. Look for curlews, oyster-catchers, wheatears, twite, snipe, golden plover, great skuas and arctic skuas.

Cross right to the fence and then walk left, down the slope, over grass and heather, to the edge of the Geo of Litlaland. From here you can glimpse the sands of Tresta and gaze across to the steep cliffs of Lamb Hoga.

Carry on left along the cliffs, where grey seals disport far below. Look for many clumps of moss campion growing at the top of the deformed conglomerate rock, dramatically exposed here. Take great care as you reach Staves Geo, a very narrow but extremely steep ravine, in which flower in great profusion roseroot, sea campion, moss campion and thrift.

Move inland a few yards to see a small lochan around which graze a dozen or more ponies with their foals. Golden plover and ringed plover call melodiously from nearby tussocks of grass. In a small pool beyond the lochan a dunlin hurries over the mud, giving its distinctive wail as it is disturbed. A snipe flies up and off to another patch of muddy ooze.

With caution, return to the cliff edge of The Snap, a mass of common scurvy grass and thrift. As you walk on, look for a magnificent natural arch that has great veins of minerals slanting through the parent rock. Both fulmars and kittiwakes nest on ledges. Continue round Butsa, over which a pair of ravens fly.

Then a narrow path leads over the turf to a fence. Follow this down until you reach the bird hide once more. Beyond, walk the waymarked path to rejoin your car.

If you have made your trip to Fetlar on a Wednesday, Thursday, Saturday or Sunday, you may wish to complete your day by visiting the Fetlar Interpretive Centre at Houbie. Here, there is a small museum, which contains much of the history of the Nicolson family. Sir Arthur Nicolson, the laird of Fetlar in the 1800s, evicted many tenants to make way for sheep.

The centre has many interesting letters and records to read and audio-visual presentations to view.

A Shetland sixern

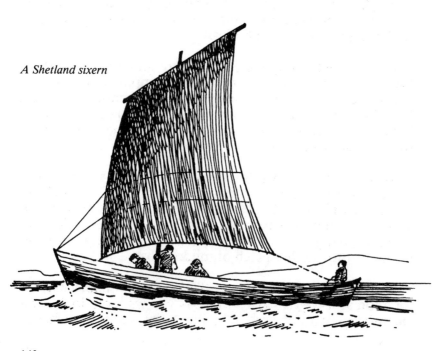

32. A Circular Walk from East of Aith, Island of Fetlar

Information

Distance: 6 miles
Time: 3-4 hours
Map: Landranger 1 Shetland, Yell and Unst
Terrain: Easy walking all the way. Watch out for the wet areas.
Parking: 645900

Enjoy this attractive walk. Take care on the steep cliffs. The road walking is free of traffic, except to the crofthouse.

To reach Fetlar, follow the instructions for Walk 31. Drive along the B9088 from the ferry and continue through Houbie, with the excellent Fetlar Interpretive Centre (Walk 31). Ignore the left turn to Aith and drive to the top of the hill to park beside a large sheep pen built of concrete blocks.

Walk back a short distance to take a track, now on your right. Stride the way as it crosses heather moorland, where many golden plover congregate and the air is filled with their haunting calls. Pass through the gate and walk towards the deserted farm of Still. This was once the island school and Fetlar's administrative centre. Today, part of the crofthouse is in ruins. Take the gate on the right before the dwelling and then continue left, maintaining the same general direction. Beyond the next gate in the fence ahead, stroll on along a sheep trod in the direction of the coast.

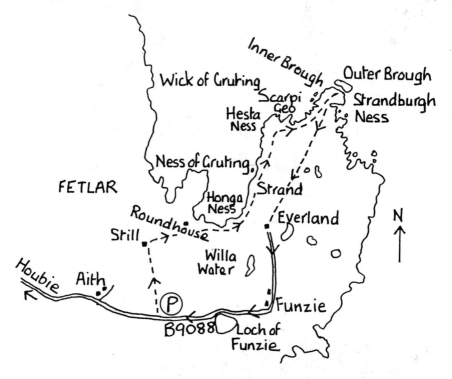

While still about a quarter of a mile from the bay, walk left to see a ruined roundhouse. This was built by Sir Arthur Nicolson (Walk 31) as a summer house, to be alone. The lower rooms were stone. Of the four entrance pillars, two are still in place and two lie forlornly on the ground. The upper storey was built of wood.

Sir Arthur set off on horseback from his home, Brough Lodge, near the ferry, to spend his first night in the summer house. As soon as he tried to sleep he was disturbed by a loud knocking, which continued until he could stand it no longer. He returned to his stately home. The minister of the kirk suggested the spirits of the people he had evicted were knocking. Later the house became an office for his factor.

From the roundhouse, enjoy the view of the pleasing fertile Gruting Valley. Wet flushes are a blaze of gold in spring, when marsh marigolds flourish. Continue to the beach and walk right. Look here for ringed plover and dunlin. Carry on, with care, along the steadily climbing cliffs, outside the fence. Look down on another glorious sandy bay and on innumerable fulmars, nesting on every available grassy ledge. Thrift and red campion colour the cliff edges.

Cross several tiny streams that hurry to tumble over the cliff edge. Walk round the end of sturdy walls. They are built of several horizontal layers of stone topped with rows laid in the vertical. Pass the roofless Smithfield House (1815) at Strand. Here lived the Smith family, but within 55 years they had gone to Australia, the house abandoned.

Red campion

Go on round the end of two more walls. Then look for a ruined watermill on a small stream, and for the snipe that enjoy the wet area. Pass a gated plantiecrub, where a blackbird nests. Be alert as you walk for the many narrow geos that slash the way.

Walk round the rock-strewn headland of Hesta Ness, from where you have a superb view of Unst, of the huge stack known as the Clett of Birrier and of Strandburgh Ness. Stroll on around Skarpi Geo, where you might spot the remains of winding gear used in quarrying soapstone a century ago. Now the way continues past more narrow precipitous geos that expose faces of conglomerate rock, some of the best in the country. Look for natural arches, caves, and stacks on which many shags stand.

Dawdle over the lovely short turf, and as you climb gently the south-facing slope of Strandburgh, look for the delicate squill turning the slope to blue. Walk to a small building at the top of the slope. Pass through the ruined walls onto the promontory of Inner Brough, where you feel as if you are almost surrounded by the ocean. Walk ahead over the grassy top, through vast patches of thrift. Be wary, and pause in good time, to view the isle of Outer Brough, to which there is no access. Between the two broughs lies the narrow Brough Sound, very far below. To the left of the island, you can glimpse a remnant of a stone wall. Here, it is believed, was a Norse monastic settlement. Today many large black-backed gulls sit and preen on large patches of scurvy grass in the sunshine.

Leave the Inner Brough and cross towards a fence that marches uphill to the skyline. The intervening pasture can be wet and more snipe feed in the ooze. Keep to the right of the fence, with heather moorland stretching away on both sides, the haunt of great and arctic skuas, curlew and whimbrel. At the brow, you can glimpse Everland farmhouse; head in that direction.

Cross the fence and stride on to keep right of a large area of reedy pools. Step through a ruined grassy wall and then over two more fences. Then walk beside a wall at the back of Smithfield. It is another wet area — where milkmaids grow and snipe and dunlin feed — so pick your way carefully.

The roundhouse

144

Take the left of two gates beyond the house and strike over the pasture to the farmhouse to join a track and then a metalled road. Continue to the settlement of Funzie and then join the B9088 as it swings right. Stride on beside the Loch of Funzie, where you may see red-throated divers, eiders, arctic terns, black-headed gulls, herring gulls, and maybe the shy red-necked phalarope. Stroll on to rejoin your car.

33. A Circular Walk from Ollaberry

Information

Distance: 3 miles
Time: 2 hours
Map: Landranger 3 Shetland, North Mainland
Terrain: Easy walking all the way.
Parking: 369806

A pleasant afternoon's stroll with a steepish climb towards the end.

To reach the picturesque hamlet of Ollaberry, leave Lerwick by the A970. Continue through Central Mainland to Voe and then on to Brae. Soon the road crosses Mavis Grind, a thin strip of land with the North Sea on the right and the Atlantic on the left — an exciting moment. After six-and-a-half miles, turn right for Ollaberry.

As you enter the hamlet, turn right immediately beyond the post office and park by the Church of Scotland. Visit the plain church, from which there is a glorious view of the bay. Look for a grandiose memorial dating from 1756, and recording the death of three children from a fever. The memorial was once attached to the gable of an earlier church.

Leave the churchyard by the gate to the parking area and pass through the gate (right) next to it. Walk over the pasture, with the wall of the church on your right, and continue along the

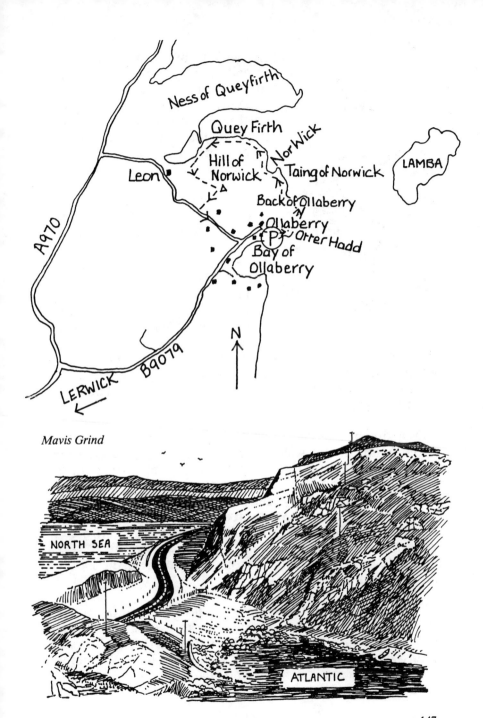

Mavis Grind

NORTH SEA

ATLANTIC

Skylark

low cliffs, which have 'scalloped' edges. In the small landslips on the edge of the cliffs tiny white lambs snooze in the sun, out of the wind. Carry on towards Otter Hadd. Enjoy the banks of primroses, spring squill and thrift. Skylarks sing continually and the tiny sandy bays below are very inviting.

Look out to see the island of Lamba, with a pristine white lighthouse on it. Then, as the way becomes steeper, and heather and bilberry grow, head up the slope to the top of the hill, known as Back of Ollaberry. From here you have a good view to the Island of Yell, over the sound. You can also see Sullom Voe Terminal, which receives crude oil from the Brent and Ninian fields. It is pumped here through long pipelines to be processed at the terminal and then sent world-wide in huge tankers. The whole complex is pleasingly unobtrusive.

Drop down the slope and walk round the promontory known as the Taing of Norwick, where the cliffs are sheer. Look for roseroot thriving in a steep ravine and butterwort in the wet flushes. Step across a burn and pass through a gate to continue above the lovely sandy bay of Nor Wick, where eiders and common gulls bathe and preen. Head on along the lower slopes of the Hill of Norwick, where wood rush grows. As you turn west along the edge of Quey Firth, you feel the sea breezes lessen as you benefit from the shelter of the Ness of the same name.

Go ahead towards the sandy ayre. It looks inviting to cross until you realise you are separated from it by a fast-flowing burn. This issues from the Loch of Queyfirth and flows up against the shallow cliffs on which you are walking. Numerous arctic terns scream overhead and many dive headlong after fish in the firth.

From here begin the steady ascent, striking diagonally left up the hill of Norwick (350 feet). It goes up relentlessly, but pause frequently for good views northwards. As you ascend, golden plovers call. Stand by the triangulation point for more superb views. Then strike west (right) to drop down, crossing several fences to join the road from Leon. Turn left and descend through pastures bright yellow with masses of primroses and marsh marigolds.

At the T-junction, turn left to walk into Ollaberry to rejoin your car. The small village has a fine 19th-century pier and crane. Here, among boulders, you might see an otter.

34. A Circular Walk from Lunna

Information

Distance: 6 miles
Time: 3 hours
Map: Landranger 2 Shetland, Whalsay
Terrain: Easy walking all the way.
Parking: 484692

An exhilarating six-miler with good views and, perhaps, at the end, coffee and scones at Lunna House.

To reach the lovely Lunna Ness, leave the A970 by the B9071, signposted Laxo-Whalsay Ferry Terminal. The road passes both piers. Continue ahead alongside Vidlin Voe to Lunna. Park on the grass verge on the left, close to the track that leads to a large well-constructed stone limekiln, shaped like a beehive, seen well in advance.

After you have visited it — beware of the nesting fulmars — return to cross the road and walk on between a tall folly high on the hill on the right and the magnificent 17th-century Lunna House to the left. The grand place is now a quiet guest house, but in the Second World War it played a great part in the 'Shetland Bus' operations. It was, until 1942, the headquarters of the Norwegian resistance movement (Walk 8).

Continue past a ruined church-like crofthouse. This was once a private chapel for the great house. Pass through a gate

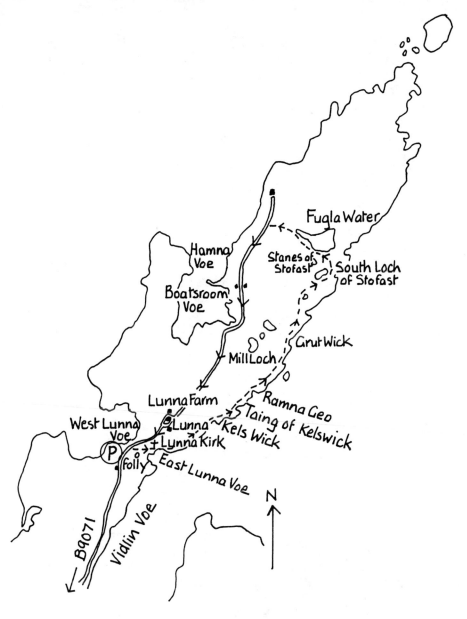

Fugla Water

Hamna Voe

Stanes of Stofast

South Loch of Stofast

Boatsroom Voe

Grut Wick

Mill Loch

Lunna Farm

Ramna Geo

West Lunna Voe

Lunna

Taing of Kelswick

Kels Wick

Lunna Kirk

P

folly

East Lunna Voe

N

Bqo71

Vidlin Voe

in the wall and bear left to visit the charming Lunna Kirk. It was
built in 1753 and is constructed of massive volcanic whinstone
blocks from nearby, with sandstone details round doors and
windows. It has two leper 'squint' holes where the afflicted

could listen to the service. Look for two ancient inscribed memorial slabs, now indecipherable, incorporated into the wall of the porch. Another recalls Robert T. Hunter of Lunna, who died in the early 1600s. The little church has a charming gallery, and on the churchyard wall an oyster-catcher nests.

Walk to the shore of East Lunna Voe and bear left to pass a ruined building, once the old smithy. Close by on the shore you might see otters and common seals. Continue along the cliffs to walk through a carpet of spring squill, with a scattering of lousewort, milkwort and tormentil. Look across to see the village of Brough on Whalsay and then the islands of Out Skerries.

Cross the wall by the stone-stepped stile, with a lovely view down into Kels Wick. Look for a large sward of primroses and the delicate mauve flower of butterwort. Take care as you round the promontory known as the Taing of Kelswick, and Ramna Geo, where a large number of fulmars nest among the violets and thrift.

Pass Mill Loch, which is set in a grassy hollow surrounded by rocky outcrops. Cross the bay of Grut Wick, where there is no trace of the Ninian oil pipeline that comes ashore here. It runs close to Lunna House and on to Sullom Voe terminal. Continue to the stile over the fence. Keep to the left side of a small lochan and stroll on. Go on over the top of a small hill, almost at the same height as the circling greater black-backed gulls. Then the attractive South Loch of Stofast lies below, with its pair of resident red-throated divers. Immediately above the loch stand the Stanes of Stofast, huge erratic boulders. These stones are believed to have been deposited by an Ice Age glacier.

Fulmar nesting

Head up the slope to stand by them — you feel like a dwarf — and then go on to drop down the slope towards the large loch of Fugla Water. Here, on several grassy islands, arctic terns nest. Walk west (left) along the loch shore, from where you have a dramatic view of the Stanes. Towards the end of the loch a pair of mallards nest on another small island.

Continue on at the head of the loch and cross several fences to reach the road. Turn left and begin the two-mile walk back to Lunna. Pass several ruined crofts and then the strange pebbly ayre that crosses half of Hamna Voe. Stride close to a small fenced area of small trees, planted in aid of Children in Need. Then carry on beside Boatsroom Voe and pass a watermill on your left.

Next comes the long climb uphill. At the brow, you can see Lunna Farm, with its pleasant trees, and Lunna House. Continue past both these and head on to rejoin your car by the limekiln.

Beehive-shaped limekiln and Lunna House

35. A Circular Walk on Out Skerries

Information

Distance:	7-8 miles
Time:	4 hours
Map:	Landranger 2 Shetland, Whalsay
Terrain:	Easy walking all the way.

A delightful round-island walk.

No visit to Shetland would be complete without a trip to the small group of islands known as the Out Skerries. They are composed of three islands: Bruray and Housay, which are connected by a bridge, and Grunay, separated from them by a narrow strip of water. On Grunay lived the lighthouse keepers who serviced the tall Out Skerries lighthouse, built in 1857 by the family firm of Stevenson. Today the light is automatic and the houses empty. The island is privately owned.

To reach these pleasing islands, a rocky 600 acres, book your ferry as soon as possible. It crosses on Friday, Saturday and Sunday only, and it takes 12 passengers and very few vehicles. The boat leaves from Vidlin on Vidlin Voe, reached first by the A970 and then by the well-signposted B9701. On the one-and-a-half hour trip, look for gannets, puffins, arctic terns, black and common guillemots and porpoises. The ferry at first keeps close to Lunna Ness and then crosses to take advantage of the shelter of Whalsay. The last stretch, into the superb natural harbour

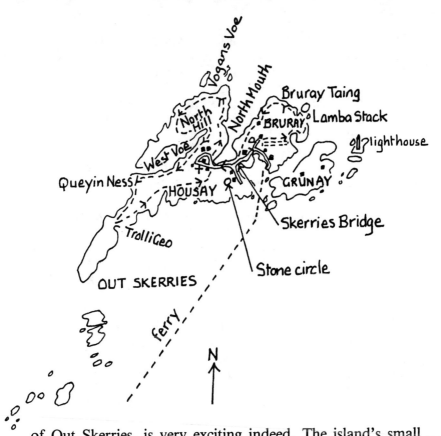

of Out Skerries, is very exciting indeed. The island's small fishing fleet berths here.

From the ferry, walk along the road and look left across the harbour to see, on a green pasture, a large stone circle, possibly Bronze Age, and known as Battle Pund. It is thought that feuds may have been settled here. Walk on along the road until just before you reach a pond, below a small reservoir. Look for the stile over the fence to your right, which you cross.

Bear right to walk above the airstrip and the aqueduct. Ahead you have a dramatic view of the lighthouse. From now on walk the lovely turf, towards the cliff edge. The way is covered with spring squill, moss campion, tormentil, daisies, violets, thrift, kidney vetch, bird's-foot trefoil, dwarf willow and red campion.

Take care as you climb steadily because the cliffs are sheer. Look over to Lamba Stack, with its innumerable fulmars. Go on around the headland, from which a magnificent view opens up across to Fetlar and Yell, with Saxa Vord on Unst showing clearly. Take care round Bruray Taing, where a grand rock garden stretches to sea level. Below, the waters of the North Sea crash white-topped on jagged rocks.

Continue along the west side of North Mouth to come to a stile in the fence on the opposite side of the small reservoir seen at the start of the walk. Strike right across great stretches of spring squill to walk round by a salmon farm where eiders congregate. Carry on to cross Skerries Bridge, built in 1957, to Housay. Now you are in the centre of the small village, where between 80 and 90 people live. Head on past the school, which at the time of writing catered for 12 children of all ages. Bear right before the coastguard hut.

Walk the few yards round the head of North Mouth, and then bear right to continue your round-island walk, again amid a glorious array of flowers. Cross the fence and stroll on. Dawdle along the east side of the huge inlet where, in bad weather, the ferry berths. Cross a pebble beach with a high shore of cobbles that stretches inland. Pass Vogans Voe, with Wether Holm across a narrow channel.

Pass through a wall and continue up the slope and on. Soon you look into West Voe, which has a large salmon farm. As you

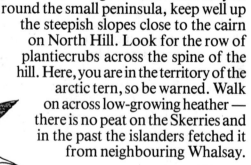

Arctic terns

round the small peninsula, keep well up the steepish slopes close to the cairn on North Hill. Look for the row of plantiecrubs across the spine of the hill. Here, you are in the territory of the arctic tern, so be warned. Walk on across low-growing heather — there is no peat on the Skerries and in the past the islanders fetched it from neighbouring Whalsay.

Climb the stile in the fence (the other end of the fence crossed earlier) and walk across old cultivation strips. Carry on to a track beside huge nets hung out to dry. They belong to the salmon farm. Walk behind the farm building, cross the fence and continue along the low cliffs, now with the salmon cages to your right.

Pass through the wall and continue round Queyin Ness, a great mass of rocky outcrops and boulders. Here, at the foot of the cliffs, the waves pound the rocks, contrasting sharply with the calm water of the voe. Great black-backed gulls glide overhead. Pass through a large area of clearance cairns and walk towards the wall on your left. Pass through it by a gap near its end. Now the promontory is very narrow and as you walk along the rocky spine great plates and jagged ridges of rock stretch away on both sides to drop to sea level.

After viewing Trolli Geo with care, and the 'island' beyond, return along the finger of land and then move to the cliffs on the right where the land broadens. Join a track faintly marked at first with tractor tyres and follow it until you reach the back of the school. Strike left behind the houses and join the road

The Out Skerries

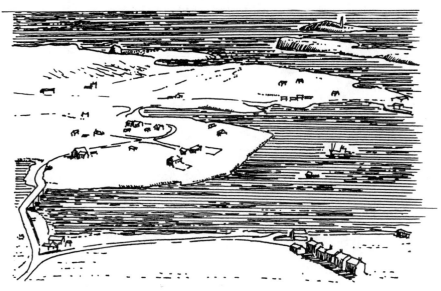

to visit Skerries Church — an attractive, beautifully-kept haven of peace.

Return along the road and just before the bridge turn right in the direction of the post office. Walk behind the houses on the right to visit the great circle of stones and ponder on their meaning.

Walk back to cross the bridge, pass the community hall and on to catch the ferry.

36. A Circular Walk on the Island of Whalsay

Information

Distance: 5 miles
Time: 3 hours
Map: Landranger 2 Shetland, Whalsay
Terrain: Easy walking all the way.
Parking: 581641

A grand walk for seaviews and for seeking out ancient sites.

The green island of Whalsay lies to the east of the Mainland of Shetland. Large and small fishing boats throng the little harbour of Symbister and around it stand many colourful houses. At the far end of the island a golf course shares its quiet remoteness with sheep, the airstrip and many nesting waders. The island probably derives its name from an old Norse word meaning Whale Island.

To reach this pleasing isle, leave the A970 just before Voe, where the ferry terminal at Laxo is well signposted. Here, another of Shetland's excellent and economic ferries takes you from Laxo to Symbister. The ferries run regularly throughout the day and the attractive journey takes 30 minutes. It is always wise to book (telephone 01806 566259).

After leaving the ferry, drive left through Symbister and take a right turn, signposted Isbister. Continue beside the loch of

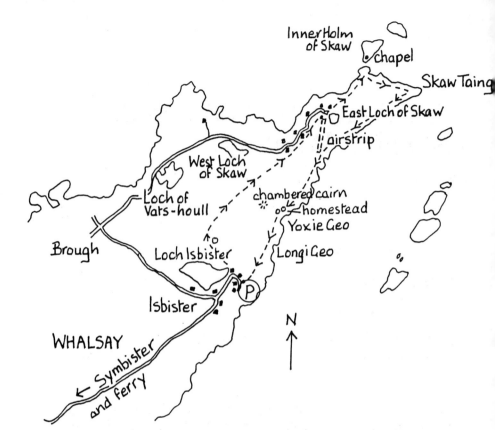

the same name and go on almost to the end of the road to park
in a large lay-by.

Walk back along the road, where the smell of burning peat
hangs in the air. When the road swings left, to the side of the
loch, stride ahead along a track, which is reinforced with gneiss.
Just before a modern bungalow at the end of the track, pass
through a gate on the left and stroll on along a grassy track.
Twelve plantiecrubs edge the way. Over to your right you can
see the sheer cliffs of the Island of Noss.

Take the right fork when the track branches and continue
climbing gently. When you reach another plantiecrub, almost
at the top of the hill, bear right and just beyond the round stone
structure look for the remains of a Neolithic chambered cairn.

It has a small rectangular hollow, lined with boulders of gneiss. Pause here and enjoy the views of the harbour and across to Ronas Hill on the Mainland. Look ahead to where the walk continues, the finger of land, north-east Whalsay, stretching out into the sea.

Dawdle along the ridge, the haunt of skylarks, wheatears, curlews and great and arctic skuas. To the east lies a series of small green islands, each with its complement of sheep. To the north-east are the Out Skerries, a small group of rocky islands, and to the north is the Island of Fetlar.

As you continue along the centre ridge look first for the Loch of Vatts-houll and then West Loch of Skaw, both to your left. Stride on over the grassy top, where much lichen and moss grows. Dunlin trill as they fly overhead. Keep to the left of the airstrip and then to the left of the small East Loch of Skaw. Shetland ponies graze nearby. Then you begin to notice the greens of the well-tended Whalsay golf course.

Go on along the pleasing low cliffs, over thrift and tormentil, until you come opposite to a small island, the Inner Holm of Skaw. Look across to see the remains of an old chapel, surrounded by large clumps of thrift. Stroll on along the wild shore, where white-topped breakers crash on the black rocks. Then continue round Skaw Taing, where a couple of turnstones stand unconcerned by the approach of humans.

Now begin to walk back along the east coast of the island, which is riven with deep geos. Here, on sunny facing cliffs, thrift, spring squill and bird's-foot trefoil flower in great profusion. Among such beauty the fulmars make their nests. Out to sea, gannets dive and a single swallow darts overhead. Ringed plovers race over the turf.

Continue beside the fence and then below the airstrip. Once past the golf course, head on along the close-cropped turf. Inland is low-growing heather. Stroll on to Pettigarth's Field, a slightly raised area, with boulders, on the slope of Yoxie Geo. Here are the remains of two buildings thought to be a Neolithic

Neolithic homesteads

homestead. In one you can trace the outlines of an entrance to two compartments.

In both houses, during excavation, broken pottery and stone tools were found. The houses were believed to have been occupied for a long period of time because of the number of grinding stones and other large tools. On the ridge immediately above is the chambered cairn visited at the start of your walk. Here this flourishing small community would have buried their dead.

Lousewort

Go on beside the fence. On the other side, where the sheep cannot graze, spring squill and thrift flower. Pass Longi Geo, where shags fly in and out. Stride on and soon the Loch of Isbister comes into view. To the left are bright green fenced fields in great

162

contrast to the rough grass of the headland. Look for the grassy track leading to where you have parked. Drop down the slope over the pretty lousewort. Keep to the right of a wall to join the track. This pleasing way is lined with red campion, bird's-foot trefoil, buttercups and flags and brings you to your car.

37. A Circular Walk from Symbister, Island of Whalsay

Information

Distance: 4½ miles
Time: 2 hours
Map: Landranger 2 Shetland, Whalsay
Terrain: Easy walking all the way.
Parking: 536625

A walk through an interesting corner of Whalsay.

To reach Whalsay, follow the instructions at the beginning of Walk 36. Leave your car near the pier. Walk west to pass Whalsay Fish, a modern fish-processing factory. Continue over the fence and head on along a track towards a quarry. Climb the slope to the right of it and press on to the side of the squat white lighthouse. Head left up the slope, inland, to a telegraph pole on the hilltop, beside which are the remains of a chambered cairn. This is a circular structure with a south-easterly entrance.

Return to the cliff edge and walk on along the pleasing way, where spring squill and thrift colour the cliff edge. Take care as you round the many geos. Look for a pair of mergansers swimming offshore. Walk on to the edge of the bay of Sand Wick, where ringed plover and dunlin race across the shore.

Move inland to the side of Sandwick Loch, passing a burnt mound. There is also a kidney-shaped burnt mound beside the

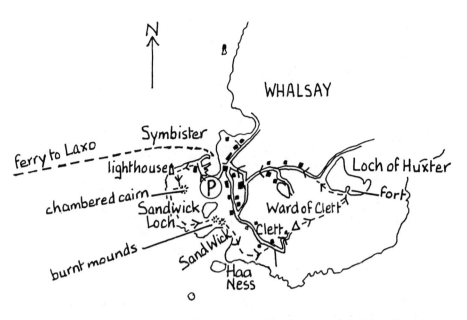

loch. Look for plantiecrubs along the shore, which is edged with flags and marsh marigolds.

From the loch you can see the fine Symbister House towering over the small town. It was built by Robert Bruce, the laird of Whalsay, in 1830. It belonged to the Bruce family until the 1920s. Today it is the local high school.

Return to the shore and then continue along the low sea cliffs. Stroll the next pebbly beach, where several turnstones congregate on a boulder covered with seaweed. Walk, with care, on along the outside of the fence on the low cliffs, through marram grass, pink campion and kidney vetch. When the cliff edge fence ends, continue over a carpet of spring squill and thrift. Cross the next fence and over Haa Ness. When you reach a wall, 50 yards before a burn, cross the fence on your left and walk over the pasture towards the houses at Clett. Pass through a farm gate and go on to a wicket gate to the road, where you turn right.

Where the road ceases to be metalled, head on. Ignore the track going off right. At a large farm building, follow the

Fort on Loch of Huxter

reinforced track as it swings left and begins to climb, zig-zagging upwards towards the triangulation point on your right, on the Ward of Clett. From here there is a glorious view. Walk on to a gated fence, passing several large disused buildings. From here you can see the 'fort' ahead and below on a small island on the Loch of Huxter.

To reach the fort, a ruined Iron-Age blockhouse, follow a faint green path down over the slopes to come to the side of the large loch, where a pair of red-throated divers utter their wailing cry. A stone causeway connects the shore with the fort. Ferns thrive in its shelter and starlings nest between the stones.

Turn left to walk the often wet way along the shore to join the road, where you proceed left. Head on along the quiet road. As you near Symbister, look for an old shop, with a flight of steps outside, on your right. Just before the shop, and well back from the road, is The Grieve House, formerly the home of Hugh McDiarmid the poet, now used as a camping bod.

Carry on to pass the Leisure Centre, where you turn right. At the T-junction turn left and then take the signposted right turn towards the ferry. On your way visit Pier House, a restored

Hanseatic bod, now used as a museum. The key is obtained from the shop opposite and there is a small entrance fee with the usual concessions.

Walk on towards the ferry to rejoin your car.

Hanseatic bod, Symbister

38. A Short Circular Walk from Neap, North Nesting

Information

Distance: 2½ miles
Time: 1 hour
Map: Landranger 3 Shetland, North Mainland
Terrain: Easy walking all the way.
Parking: 501583

A pleasing short walk.

The greenness of the pastures about Brettabister, Housabister, Kirkabister and the Hill of Neap are in great contrast to the heather-clad slopes of much of North Nesting.

To reach this tranquil corner of central mainland, leave the A970 by the B9075 at Catfirth, and continue on the B-road until you reach the memorial at Brettabister. Here, turn right to drive to the end of the road, and park tidily, away from gates. Walk north (left), along a reinforced track through sheep pastures and where ponies graze.

Green plover or lapwing

Before the fence, bear right and walk over the lovely turf to the edge of the cliffs. Turn right and walk south across Valla Ness. Curlew,

North Nesting

Loch of Kirkabister
Housabister
Brettabister
B9075
broch
Valla Ness
Wick of Neap
Hog Island
Hill of Neap
Stany Hog
The Keen
Ura Stack
P
N

oyster-catcher and green plover fly overhead, calling. Continue round the Wick of Neap, with its two small bays. Thrift, primrose, pink campion and spring squill colour the way. Common seals peer from the water. Look for two ancient grassy nousts on the shore.

Go on along the glorious way and peer carefully over the intervening narrow channel to Hog Island and Stany Hog — the latter very stony. Here, innumerable shags nest on dark ledges close to the heaving sea. Fulmars brood their eggs and young, in vast numbers.

Carry on around The Keen, below the Hill of Neap, and walk on past Ura Stack. Tread warily round the sheer cliffs of a small bay and press on to the fence, which you can cross at the end nearest the great hollow. Then descend steadily to sea level, where ringed plover race across the turf and the shore.

Where a small burn tumbles through the pastures, turn inland. After 50 yards, cross the stream and follow a turf and stone wall. Then step over it and head towards a gate in the wall ahead. This gives access to the road, where you turn right to rejoin your car.

Before you leave this quiet corner of Shetland, you might wish to visit the church at Housabister. Just behind the church stands a pile of stones on a grassy mound — the remains of a broch.

Housabister Church

39. A Circular Walk from Setter, Weisdale

Information

Distance: 3½ miles
Time: 2 hours
Map: Landranger 3 Shetland, North Mainland
Terrain: Easy walking all the way.
Parking: 397547

An inland expedition providing a great contrast to the many cliff walks of Shetland.

Rookery

To reach Setter, leave the A970 by the B9075, heading west. At Setter the B-road makes a sharp left turn, but continuing ahead is a cart track. A short distance along this is a lay-by for two cars, off the track, and before a gate.

Beyond the gate, walk ahead. Then bear right to pass a ruined crofthouse and go on towards a small plantation of firs and pines — a rare sight in Shetland. Walk uphill by the fence, with the trees to your right. From the

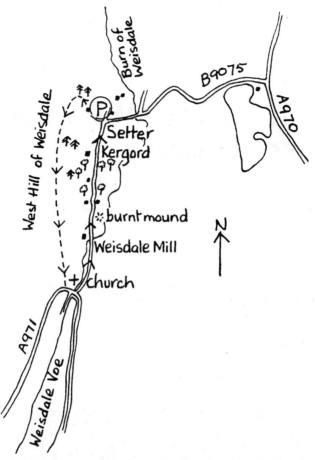

conifers comes a strange sound for the islands, the caco-
phony of a rookery. On the edge of the pines grow several
hawthorn bushes.

At the end of the plantation, turn left and stroll on along
the same contour. Ahead you can see Fitful Head at the
southern end of Mainland. Continue on to walk above a
second plantation, where pine and larch grow. Stride on to
a third, planted with a band of rowan, alder and birch edging
mature conifers.

Walk on along a turf wall, past a row of ruined crofthouses,
then along an old ruined trackway, which must have linked all
the houses and probably led down to the church. Head for the

gabled church at the head of Weisdale Voe by dropping diagonally left, crossing fences by gates and continuing to the B-road just before it joins the A971. Turn left and visit the 19th-century church.

Go on along the quiet road to Weisdale Mill. This was built in 1855. Water from the dam, across the road, drove the mill, which served a large area. The grain for milling was brought in boats to the head of the voe and then transported inland. Today the mill has been converted into an art gallery with regular exhibitions. The ground floor is for the display of spinning and weaving and an area for refreshments. Alas, all the old machinery has long gone and therefore the mill cannot be restored to its past glory.

Stroll on and just before the farm, at the start of the last pasture on the right, look for a burnt mound, large enough for cooking — and perhaps for saunas. Beyond the farm, in more woodland, is another rookery, this time set high in sycamores.

Then you pass the many trees about Kergord House, planted in the 19th century. Look for elm, copper beech, sycamore, rowan, ash, willow, whitebeam and horse chestnut. Below

Trees at Kergord

them flowers a vast carpet of celandines and pink purslane. Here in the trees a migrant, Blyth's reed warbler, on its way to Finland, flits about the lower branches of a sycamore.

Stroll on past the 19th-century laird's house. Once it was known as Flemington and the mill, just passed, was part of the estate. The house was built of stone from the crofthouses emptied during the Clearances. In 1940 it became the administrative centre for the activities of the 'Shetland Bus'. In 1945 the house was renamed Kergord.

Go along the road to rejoin your car.

40. A Trail through Lerwick

Information

Distance: 4½ miles
Time: 2-3 hours, or as much time as you have
Terrain: Easy walking.

A grand way to spend a fine or wet day.

Lerwick, the capital and administrative centre of Shetland, dates from the 17th century. It owes its existence to the splendid deep natural harbour of Bressay Sound. Its name comes from the Norse meaning 'muddy (or clay) bay'.

1. Park in the Victoria Pier car park. The pier was built in 1860. As you leave, look for the Diana fountain, a memorial to the whaling ship *Diana* which became trapped for six months in Arctic ice (1866-67). When the ship did return 13 of the crew were dead, nine of them from Shetland.

2. Cross the road to the flagged Market Cross (place of proclamations) where a water pump once stood. Turn left and walk along the flagged Commercial Street, which is lined with small shops. Pass in front of the sturdy Bank of Scotland and the Post Office.

3. Cross, with care, the busy Church Road and walk ahead along the continuing Commercial Street. Pass the Queen's Hotel, which has incorporated into it two lodberries, small stone jetties built by merchants who lived in the houses. The

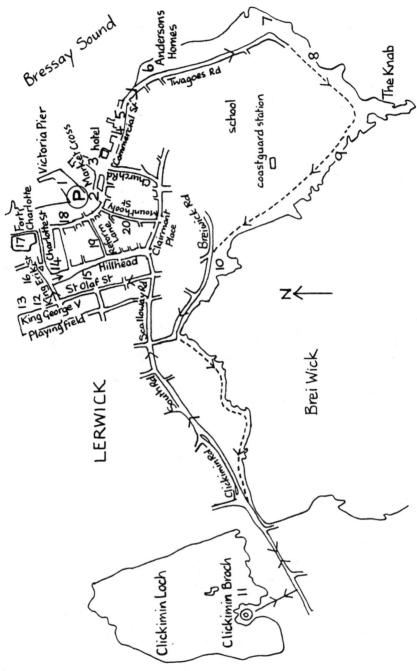

Bressay Sound

LERWICK

Victoria Pier

Market Cross

3 hotel

Commercial St.

Andersons Homes

6

7

8

The Knab

Twagoes Rd

school

coastguard station

9

Fort Charlotte

17

16

13

12

King Erik St

2

Charlotte St

8

Reform Lane

19

Mounthooly St

20

Church Rd

Clairmont Place

Breiwick Rd

10

P

15

St Olaf St

Hillhead

King George V

Playing field

N

Scalloway Rd

Southroad

Clickimin Rd

Brei Wick

Clickimin Loch

Clickimin Broch

11

latter were also used as warehouses where goods could be unloaded directly from boats.

4. Walk on to look over the low wall bordering Bain's Beach, to see two fine lodberries. The very small sandy bay is named after a 19th-century carpenter. Here, smugglers' tunnels run under the street. At the end of the tiny bay, steps lead down to the beach.

5. Look over the wall of the next bay for a good view of more lodberries. Continue along the pleasing flagged way past Stout's Court. Just beyond stands the 17th-century Old Manse — the oldest occupied house in Lerwick.

6. Stroll on past The Knowe and its quaint garage, which has an upturned boat for a roof. Then pass on your left the Arthur Anderson House for widows of seamen, now converted to flats. The founder was a famous Shetlander who built the house in memory of his wife. He was Member of Parliament for the islands and founder of Shetland's first newspaper.

7. Go ahead along the continuing footpath, signposted The Knab. Enjoy the magnificent view across the sound to the island of Bressay and its prominent lighthouse. Look for ringed plover probing for prey among the boulders below and for rafts of eider floating offshore. Listen for fulmars calling quietly to each other as they settle onto their ledges.

8. Continue past remnants of wartime defence buildings and then below the cemetery. Walk up the steadily climbing path to the rocky prominence known as The Knab, where the sea is eroding its steep sides and thrift flowers in vast numbers.

9. Pass through the kissing-gate and go on along the footpath signposted Breiwick Road. To the right is the old golf course, with the coastguard station above. Continue around Breiwick Bay to join Breiwick Road. Walk left. Pass the attractive grey stone houses on the right and a greensward on the left.

Clickimin Broch

10. Carry on along the continuing footpath, signposted Ayre of Clickimin. At the road turn left and walk along Clickimin Road. At Sound Garage, cross the road and pass through a kissing-gate. This gives access to a causeway that leads to Clickimin Broch. The broch was built on an islet in the freshwater Clickimin Loch. In the 19th century the water level was lowered and as a result the broch now stands on a promontory. However, it is still approached by a causeway because of the boggy nature of the ground.

11. Wander at will around the striking structure. It was occupied from about 700 BC and was a Bronze Age farmhouse, then an Iron Age farmhouse. Later it was developed as a broch. Later still it became a wheelhouse settlement, or aisled house.

12. Return to the road, turn left and walk back along Clickimin Road and the continuing South and Scalloway Roads. Turn left into Saint Olaf Street and walk until you come to King George's playing fields. Go in and watch the bowling, putting or tennis. Sit in the sun and enjoy the colourful immaculate gardens.

13. Then walk on past the children's play area to part of the same field where, in late January, a replica of a Viking longship galley is burned during Up Helly Aa, the annual fire festival.

14. Walk back a short distance to go up King Erik Street towards the granite war memorial. Behind, and towering over it, is the splendid Town Hall (1882) with its turrets, tower, corbie-stepped gables, crenellated walls and stained glass windows.

15. Walk right, in front of the memorial, along Lower Hillhead to the library. Outside is a massive propeller blade from the *RMS Oceanic* that went down off Foula in 1914. Above the library is the museum. Go inside and see the many well-arranged, fascinating exhibits of Shetland's past and present.

16. Return past the memorial and walk right to pass on your left the stately County Buildings (1875). Beside them is the police station. To your right is a signpost directing you to Fort Charlotte. Pass the Garrison Theatre and enter the main gate of the fort.

17. The fort was built in 1665 by the master mason to Charles II. It was reconstructed in 1781-82 as a coastal defence

Lerwick harbour

179

fort during the American War of Independence. It was named after George III's queen. Walk over the grass for a splendid view of Bressay Sound.

18. Leave by the south gate and turn left down Charlotte Street. Turn right to walk along Commercial Street past more houses with corbie gables and many chimneys. Notice the several intriguing stepped lanes climbing up to the right. Rich and poor lived in these lanes in the 19th century. They were steep and overcrowded but protected the inhabitants from the bitter winds. Pass the Grand Hotel (1887) and ascend Reform Lane, named after the Reform Act of 1832.

19. Towards the top of the lane, look for a garden of trees where a blackbird sings. Turn left at the end and walk along Hillhead and then turn left into Clairmont Place.

20. Turn left again into Mounthooly Street. Walk down the lane through which, in the 18th century, a stream flowed. Just before The Lounge public house, walk left behind the building to the foot of Law Lane. Here the sheriff and various lawyers lived in the 19th century. Walk back to Mounthooly Street and continue downhill to Market Cross to rejoin your car.

41. A Circular Walk on Aith Ness, Bressay

Information

Distance: 4 miles
Time: 2 hours
Map: Landranger 4 Shetland, South Mainland
Terrain: Easy walking all the way. Care required on the cliffs.
Parking: 511427

A grand walk with dramatic cliffs and good views.

The island of Bressay lies three-quarters of a mile east of Lerwick, across the Bressay Sound. The shelter it provides has given Lerwick a fine natural harbour. The island's population of about 370 live on the west coast, looking across to the capital. It was not always so. Three times as many people lived on the island early in the last century, mainly on the east coast, but they were cleared in the 1870s to make room for sheep.

The island is composed mainly of Old Red Sandstone and from this rock the many walls are constructed. They enclose the narrow roads, and in summer the verges are bright with colourful flowers.

A frequent, regular and inexpensive ferry leaves from Albert Building in the centre of Lerwick, just north of Shetland Islands Tourism. It takes five minutes to cross the sound to Maryfield. As you drive from the terminal you see to your left a grand

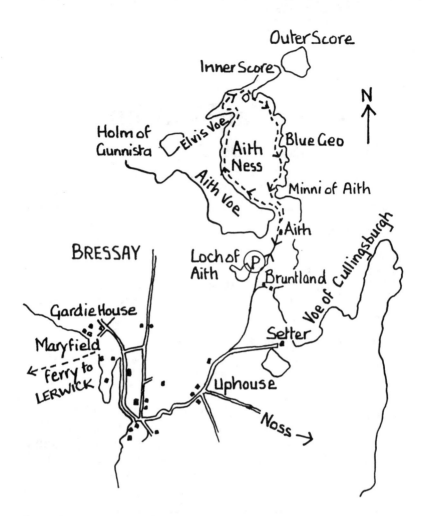

Georgian dwelling, built in 1724, known as Gardie House and occupied by the present laird.

To reach Aith Ness, follow the signpost for Noss. At Uphouse, ignore the right turn for the small island and continue ahead in the direction of Setter. When the farmhouse comes into view, drive along an unsignposted reinforced track, going off left through heather moorland. Park in a reinforced area at Bruntland, a crofthouse that stands to your right, close to the Loch of Aith.

Walk on along the track, to pass through a gate. Beyond, head over left to follow a good sheep trod (which continues all round the Ness) over the shallow cliffs of Aith Voe, where, earlier in this century, herring was processed into fishmeal. Today the voe supports a salmon farm.

Hard fern

Carry on over the short turf, where spring squill, tormentil, silverweed, violet, bird's-foot trefoil, kidney vetch and thrift flourish. Go round a small bay to pass a ruined house and the remains of fortifications used in the First World War. Just offshore lies the Holm of Gunnista. Among the heather, in the shelter of deserted rabbit burrows, delicate hard fern thrives and here, too, you might find the nest of a curlew with its three or four large eggs.

Continue round Elvis Voe, where the thin, layered sandstone forms a flat path, and stroll on over a carpet of thrift. Just before you reach the islands of Inner Score and Outer Score, look in the cliffs for fascinating conglomerate rock with granite and quartzite embedded in the sandstone.

Now you begin to walk the east coast of the Ness. Cross a delightful ayre with turquoise water over sand on the seaward side and a deep blue lochan on the other. On both sides of the ayre eiders swim. Then, begin the climb up the cliffs of Score Hill, where fulmars nest among the thrift that grows on the ledges. Closer to the sea a row of shags preen. Continue with care to walk round the Blue Geo, where sandstone was quarried. It was used to pave the streets of Lerwick and for building and roofing. Lerwick Town Hall is built with Bressay stone. The quarry is now the haunt of herring gulls and many have their nests here — beds of heather, grass and moss.

Stride on around the Minni of Aith. To your right, arctic terns wheel and more herring gulls nest. Here, too, an eider sits close on its nest — how will the young run the gauntlet of the gulls to reach the sea?

Drop down the slope to pass through and beside the well-built walls of a ruined crofthouse (Aith) and go on until you rejoin the track. Here, a herring gull carries a piece of seaweed attached to which is a mussel. This the bird drops repeatedly until the shell breaks and the flesh can be eaten. Stroll on with the Loch of Aith to your right from where redshanks and ringed plovers call from their heathery environs.

Walk on to rejoin your car.

Traditional interior of crofthouse

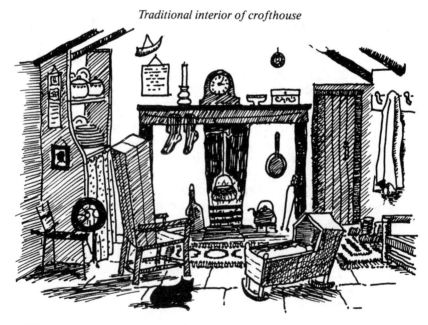

42. A Circular Walk from Kirkabister Lighthouse on the Isle of Bressay

---

Information

Distance: 9 miles
Time: 5 hours
Map: Landranger 4 Shetland, South Mainland
Terrain: Generally easy walking. Strong shoes required for the wet areas.
Parking: 489378

An excellent trek with some road walking — never unpleasant in Shetland.

To reach the Isle of Bressay follow the instructions at the start of Walk 41. Drive from the ferry and take the first right turn. Just beyond a sharp turn in the road take the next right turn, signposted Kirkabister. Continue to the end of the road to park. You are asked not to block the turning point.

Ahead is the lighthouse, built on this southern tip of the island in 1858 by the Stevenson family. It is fully automated now and is a welcoming sight when approaching Lerwick through the Bressay Sound.

Just beyond the lighthouse is the wreck of the Russian klondyker, the *Lunokhod*. Pass through the gate to the left of the lighthouse and begin the steady climb over the flower-covered

turf. Look left to see a ruined settlement, with old walls and turf dykes, on the slopes above. Look back for a good view of the wreck and the lighthouse and of a splendid natural arch. Ahead you can see Sumburgh Head.

Old fishing boat

Continue upwards, with the fence to the right, where wood rush grows. Look over the glorious busy sound. You can see large boats being re-fuelled, a huge red tanker standing at anchor, small fishing boats puttering through the sound, a speedboat racing back and forth and several helicopters flying over the water. Beyond stands Lerwick, an attractive grey and red stone town with houses climbing up hills and ending neatly at the edge of the frowning moorland.

After the long pull up The Ord (542 feet), pause again to enjoy the pleasing view. Here, the impressive cliffs are much eroded. Continue on over the heather, where great skuas fly and golden plover call evocatively. Then descend steadily, keeping beside the cliffside fence until you reach a wall. Walk inland to go through the gate. Beyond, descend over grass to pass a ruined homestead and sheep pen and cross the Burn of Veng, which drops seawards in small falls. Then cross the thyme-edged burn that flows out of Sand Vatn. It cascades downhill in more lively falls — both burns continue to the cliff edge and plummet in white tresses to the sea.

Stroll on over The Bard, which juts finger-like out into the sea. At Bard Head, surrounded by vast clumps of thrift, stands a huge rusting gun from the First World War. Close by, at the cliff edge, is all that remains of the gantry that hauled it up. Walk on along the grassy headland to view Stoura Clett, with its fine arch. Look for puffins here and, as usual, numerous fulmars. Roseroot grows about the cliffs. Then carry on to the small Loch of Seligeo, with the dramatic Seli Geo away to the right. Out at sea gannets fly, and eiders coo and idle on the water far below. Across Noss Sound lies the lovely island of Noss.

As you begin to descend, ringed plover scurry over the turf like clockwork mice. Continue round a bay where sandstone flags lie in a huge tumble, remnants of earlier quarrying. Go round the next geo, which really is just a bonny rock garden, and then climb the steep slopes ahead.

As you walk, listen for snipe whirring overhead and look for ravens flying high above. Continue on in the direction of a ruined crofthouse, above the Loch of Grimsetter. Then walk inland on the same contour line to cross the wall. Continue to a dozen or more ruined crofthouses, a sad reminder of the days of the Clearances. At the back of the one nearest to the loch, look for the souterrain, an earth house. It has a stone lintel over an opening two feet high. Get on your knees to look along the passage to see fine walls, shelves and gables.

All around this glorious corner grows a vast flower garden of orchids and lousewort. In the loch great skuas and black-backed gulls bathe. Head on, diagonally left, to a gate in the wall. Beyond lies a good track well reinforced. Stride on to the side of the Loch of Brough, where red-throated divers swim serenely. Half-way along, turn left and climb the slope beside a drainage ditch, walking a grassy swathe through the heather moorland. As you reach the top of the slope the ground can be wet but you very soon join the road.

Turn left and follow it to the end. Pass through a gate and drop down the slope to cross another wet area where wild iris grows about a small burn, and then walk on to join the access track to Ward Hill (742 feet), which supports a television mast. Here turn right and walk downhill to join a road. Turn left and stroll the quiet mile-and-a-half to the lighthouse, enjoying the colourful array of wild flowers that fill the verges and ditches along the way.

Kirkabister Lighthouse and wreck of Lunokhod

43. A Circular Walk round the Island of Noss

Information

Distance: 4-5 miles

Time: 3 hours

Map: Landranger 4 Shetland, South Mainland, or the map in the leaflet provided by the centre

Terrain: Easy walking but immense care is required on the cliffs.

Parking: 528411

A magnificent walk, with glorious views and much birdlife.

The walk round Noss is special. If you are interested in birds it is extra special. The island is owned by the Garth Estate, and jointly managed by Scottish Natural Heritage. It is home to 400 Shetland ewes and during the lambing season these are brought inside the Hill Dyke to avoid disturbing the breeding of great skuas.

The rocks of the island are Old Red Sandstone and this lies horizontally on the cliffs. As these weather, innumerable ledges are created, just right for the birds to nest and close to their feeding grounds. Here thrive 7,000 pairs of gannets, 6,000 pairs of fulmars, 7,000 pairs of kittiwakes and 40,000 guillemots. You will also see many puffins, shags, black guillemots, great black-backed gulls, razorbills, herring gulls, dunlin, turnstones, golden plover, ringed plover and ravens. On the heather

moorland great skuas rule, often in conflict with their smaller
cousins, the arctic skuas.

Noss can be visited from mid-May until mid-August, when a
warden is present. It is closed on Mondays and Thursdays.
To reach this bird kingdom, follow the directions for Bressay
(Walk 41), then drive across the island following the signpost
directions for Noss. Leave your car in the car park at the top of
the last hill and walk down the track to the tiny jetty. Wait here
for an inflatable dinghy to come across Noss Sound. The
warden is most vigilant and your waiting time is short. If the sea
is too rough for a crossing a red flag is flown. Make sure you
have suitable clothing and strong shoes or boots — the rocks
can be slippery when clambering into and out of the boat.

The house used by the warden and his staff is called Gungstie
and dates from the 17th century. There is a small information
room. Outside look for the restored beehive-shaped drying kiln
and also the restored 19th-century pony-pund. These buildings
were leased by the Marquis of Londonderry to breed Shetland
pony stallions used in his coal-mines after 1842 when an Act of
Parliament banned children and women from working there.
There is an interpretative display.

The island has been inhabited for 4,000 years. The Vikings arrived in the ninth century and the name Noss comes from the Norse for 'a point of rock'. The Jamieson family lived on the island from 1904 until 1939, Noss's last permanent residents.

Great skua and arctic skua

Leave the house and walk round the lovely sandy bay of Nesti Voe. Strike diagonally right towards the turf dyke and continue to the ladder-stile over the wall. Inland, skylarks, twites, wheatears and golden plover seem unconcerned by the many great skuas. From the low cliffs a pair of eider usher their four dark-feathered ducklings towards the sea.

Pass through an old wall and the remains of a building. Continue over a carpet of thrift and then begin the steady climb upwards, with the remains of an old wall running along the edge of the cliffs. As you walk you realise the wall goes on and on — how reassuring when you are peering from on high. In the 19th century it took Robert Morrison two years to build and he was paid seven old pence a fathom (six feet), using the stone of the island. Before its construction, the children of the island kept the cattle from straying too close to the dangerous edges.

Continue round the Point of Hovie, where many fulmars nest among the lovely rock garden of sea campion, red campion, moss campion and thrift. Then, as you continue climbing, you come to Cradle Holm (600 feet), a grassy-topped stack where once a 'cradle' on two cables was used to carry men and sheep across. Others used the cradle to collect eggs and feathers. The contraption was removed in 1864. Today the stack is a haven for thousands of guillemots, which sit with their faces to the cliff, and for razorbills, which sit apart and in very small numbers. On top a large number of great black-backed gulls nest among the scurvy grass.

The Noup of Noss

As you walk on along the cliffs look for a Shetland wren nesting in the wall and a few kittiwakes breeding on the ledges. Here you might see your first puffin — though keep alert because these birds bob back quickly into the rabbit burrow they have commandeered. As you walk round Charlie's Holm, you may see more puffins, the top of the stack pitted with burrows and covered with droppings.

Then as you move on the great gannetry on Rumble Wick and The Noup comes into view. Here the huge cliff-faces are white with guano and thousands of gannets sit patiently on their ledges. Birds constantly fly in and out and others plunge, swim and preen. The smell is very strong. Below the gannets, row after row of guillemots breed. Deeper down in the hollows and caves shags nest.

Keep beside the wall to reach the triangulation point on The Noup (700 feet). From here you can see Unst, Fetlar, Yell, Whalsay, Bressay and the Mainland. Then begin the gradual but unrelenting descent to pass several dramatic geos, all packed with guillemots and fulmars. Look for the lovely roseroot colouring the cliff faces.

Follow the footpath sign, which directs you away from a very contorted red sandstone geo, and continue along North Croo. Look for various waders and for black guillemots, which mew to each other from the cliffs.

Climb the ladder-stile and follow the wall, keeping to the north of the Hill of Papilgeo. Cross the Hill Dyke to pick up your outward path to the visitor centre.

44. A Circular Walk on the Island of Mousa

Information	
Distance:	4 miles
Time:	All the time between boats
Map:	Landranger 4 Shetland, South Mainland
Terrain:	Easy walking. Very narrow steps lead to the top of the broch.
Parking:	437249

An exciting boat trip to a very interesting island.

A walk on Mousa is a joy — not just to see the famous broch, but the birds, seals, wild flowers, a homestead, and a burnt mound. The boat trip is fun too.

Leave Lerwick by the A970, southbound. After 15 miles, turn left at the sign for Sandwick, Hoswick, and the Mousa ferry. Continue down the narrow road for half a mile to the attractive cobbled pier. There is ample parking and good facilities.

A regular summer boat service is operated, weather permitting, by Tom Jamieson. (Telephone 01950 431367 to book, and to confirm the trip on the day.) The trip, on the *M/B Solan III*, takes 15 minutes. From the boat porpoises are often seen and the occasional otter, minkie and killer whale. Groups of seabirds seen include guillemots, shags, black guillemots, razorbills and puffins.

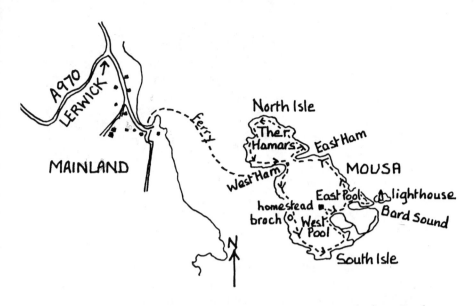

The isle of Mousa no longer has a human population. In the 18th century, 11 families lived on the isle, but the last residents left in the 1860s.

The broch is one of the tall dry-stone, hollow-wall towers unique to Scotland, built by Iron-Age farmers about 2,000 years ago. It is extremely well preserved and stands to near its original height of 43 feet, startlingly high when you stand inside and look up.

It may have been built as an occasional strong point for the local community, but the small chambers inside suggest that it was later made into a dwelling. The chambers are arranged around a pool of water. There are galleries, an internal staircase and a parapet.

The broch has had two famous couples as tenants. In 900 AD a couple eloping from Norway to Iceland were shipwrecked on the island. They married and spent the winter in the broch. The other couple were the mother of Harald, Earl of Orkney, and her lover. They took refuge in the broch and the furious earl laid siege to it, unsuccessfully. He eventually gave up and went away.

Today the broch is wonderfully peaceful and the only tenants are the storm petrels. The strange churring noise you may hear is their song. These tiny swallow-like birds, which are well adapted to life at sea, are not agile on land. They can come ashore only after sunset, to brood their young, safe from predation by gulls and skuas.

Storm petrels

Leave the boat and head south (right) over blue squill and tormentil. As you pass a huge boulder beach you are asked to walk on the turf because the petrels nest between the boulders and are very sensitive to interference. They will desert their eggs or chicks if disturbed.

From the broch walk inland to the nearest point of a small loch to see a burnt mound. Return to the coast to walk the magnificent coastline, where red sandstone tilts towards the sea. Large beds of scurvy grass, sea campion and thrift provide picturesque sites for nesting fulmars.

Continue over a small hill, which is covered with a glorious carpet of thrift. Further on you come to an area where much sandstone has been removed and used for paving stones in Lerwick. The builders of the broch used sandstone from the same site.

At the tidal West Pool with a beach of shell-sand, sit and watch the antics of the many common and grey seals. Eiders swim and coo. In the damp hinterland of the pool grow pink orchids and masses of primroses, and among these a colony of arctic terns nest. Tread warily because the eggs and chicks are difficult to spot. Walk with your map on your head to protect yourself from the aerial attacks of these ferocious protectors of their young.

Follow the wall along inland to visit the site of an ancient homestead. You can just see the stones that delineated a passage between two dwellings.

Return to West Pool and then continue on to East Pool, where more seals haul out and others sing and blow. Beyond the lovely bay, walk out to look over Bard Sound and glimpse Mousa lighthouse with its jetty.

Dawdle along the lovely cliffs to see a huge raft of male eiders. Take care as you round a natural arch-cum-blowhole at the landward side of a deep geo. It lies at the end of a wall, so walk a short distance inland before continuing. Skylarks carol and wheatears flit about boulders.

Just before you stroll on around East Ham onto the North Isle, look for black guillemots on the boulders close to the water. Here, too, shags dry their wings. On North Isle heather grows and in the damper areas butterwort, milkwort, orchids and lousewort flower. Now you run the gauntlet of another tern colony. Two pairs of arctic skuas zoom through the screeching birds and then settle a short way off and watch. On The Hamars a pair of great skuas sit. Far below more seals peer upwards.

Carry on around the cliffs to the jetty.

Mousa Broch

45. A Circular Walk on Fair Isle

Information

Distance: 8 miles
Time: The time between flights
Map: Landranger 4 Shetland, South Mainland
Terrain: Easy walking. A steep climb up to the top of Ward Hill.

A magical day's walking.

Fair Isle, three miles long and a mile wide, lies 23 miles from Sumburgh Head. In 1948 the island was bought by George Waterston, who thus achieved a dream that had helped him survive the rigours of being a prisoner of war. In 1954 he handed over the island to the National Trust for Scotland, who still own it.

There are two ways of reaching this beautiful island. One, extremely inexpensive, is by the boat the *Good Shepherd IV,* usually from Grutness. This trip takes two-and-a-half hours — but you cannot return on the same day. It is an exhilarating and sometimes rough crossing with much to see in the way of porpoises, dolphins and seabirds, The other way, and fairly costly, is to travel by Loganair. The journey takes 25 minutes and it too is a wonderful experience. You see the cliffs of both the mainland and the island 'from the outside, looking in'. During the summer you can fly on Monday, Wednesday and Friday, and have on average six-and-a-half hours on the island — just time for a great walk.

The plane lands on an airstrip used during the Second World War. The wheels touch down on clumps of thrift and the plane sends great skuas on their way. There is a waiting room and toilet by the airstrip. Walk round the perimeter until opposite the facilities and begin the long climb up a reinforced track. This comes to a very obvious British Telecom mast, built on the site of an old crofthouse. From here follow a grassy groove straight to the top of Ward Hill (712 feet), where there is a walled triangulation point and the debris of a wartime radar station. Enjoy the wonderful view of the whole island and of

Sumburgh Head, Fitful Head, Bressay and Noss. Here, men watched for the dreaded press gang, racing off to hide in caves on Malcolm's Head, facing Fogli Stack. Later men watched for U-boats in the First World War.

Walk north (right), with care along the cliffs, over crowberry, dwarf willow and tormentil. Then drop down the slope in the direction of the north lighthouse across the mossy turf. Above, a snipe flies high and fast, drumming as it goes. Cross the Burn of Wirrvie on concrete blocks and climb up between two small hills, where a pair of twite call sweetly as they peck about the turf.

Continue to a small lochan. A great skua and many immature black-backed gulls bathe. Walk right beside the pool, over thrift, and beside the remains of the old north-south dyke — an ancient wall. Continue to a narrow road, walking over young bracken. Turn left and dawdle past the black Golden Water, where tufted ducks idle. Carry on along the road to pass a great blowhole, linked to the sea by a long subterranean passage. Around its quarry-like slopes flower thrift, kidney vetch and sea campion. You can see these from behind the rails of the road, but not the water in the bottom.

Before the lighthouse, strike over left, warily, to the edge of the cliffs. Here, in early summer, a memorable sight awaits. Puffins sit close to your feet. Fulmars fill almost every ledge on the sandstone cliff face. Guillemots, by the hundreds, stand in line with faces to the wall on ledges far down. Razorbills find gaps between the guillemots. Shags fly to the lower darker part of the great cliffs. Out on a great white stack and cliffs there is a large gannetry, which began to form in 1975. Far below, on the sea, float great rafts of guillemots and razorbills. There is constant movement as an enormous number of birds fly to and from their nest sites and their rich feeding grounds out at sea. Grey seals peer upwards.

Return to the road and continue to the lighthouse, built in 1891, now fully automated, the houses empty. Then begin to walk south, along the lovely cliffs, which are cloudy blue with squill. Now the great hole is to your right. Here, on the tops of the cliffs, sit puffins about their burrows, and beyond, on cliff faces and on the water far below are a vast number of birds.

Stroll on to sit on the edge of slightly lower cliffs and watch more puffins busy in and out of their burrows. Look down on kittiwakes, snowy white birds with pale grey mantles, black tipped. They sail on the air currents and then return to their nests on the steepest of slopes on the cliffs, or in the caves below. Watch the shags circling with trailing stems of seaweed for their untidy nests.

Leave the cliff and drop down the slope to cross the burn. Climb up the other side to join the road. Turn left and continue along the road. Here, meadow pipits and skylarks rise, filling the air with song. As the road winds round left, walk inland to Ferni-Cup to see two burnt mounds, part of what is believed to be a Bronze-Age settlement. Return to the road and stride on where overhead hundreds of terns circle their nests on the rolling shallow hills inland, and more snipe rise from the wet areas beside the road.

Dawdle round the corner to come to the bird observatory, which collects and analyses data on birds. George Waterston

Fair Isle Bird Observatory

first established an observatory in the old naval station at North Haven. Today the new buildings, opened in 1969, comprise an observatory and a lodge, which offers fine accommodation. Continue behind the observatory, swinging left to visit the glorious stretch of sand at North Haven. Here you might see the *Good Shepherd IV* in her giant noust blasted out of the side of Bu Ness, and the breakwater protecting the small harbour.

Return past the observatory and make a detour to see, on a promontory, an early Iron-Age fort with ramparts guarding its entrance. From now on you pass many of the nets used by the observatory for ringing and data collection. Look left, and if you have time, cross the stile and walk over to see Sheep Craig (443 feet). The huge grass-topped stack is linked to the island by an isthmus. Sheep and men were once winched by chains to its smooth turf.

Look for prostrate juniper hugging the slopes to your right and pink orchids growing among the heather — the latter a pink haze in August. Pass more nets. On your right a small group of willows, sycamore and firs are half-covered with nets. This most productive trap is situated in the Gully of Funniquoy. Above, on the Burn of Gilsetter, are the ruins of several watermills.

Go on along the road and then on your right is a turn that leads very quickly to the airstrip. Hopefully you have time left to stroll towards the south of the island, where the Fair Islanders live.

Go on and look for the hill dyke, a long straight dry-stone wall that almost divides the island in two, separating the heather moor to the north and the crofts and green fields to the south. Beside it you can see traces of a much older dyke, 'Feelie Dyke', with remnants of turf-covered stone.

Continue on the way where, in the ditches, you can see marsh marigolds, milkmaids, water mint and later ragged robin and forget-me-nots. Above right is another huge colony of arctic terns circling and screeching as arctic skuas dive and wheel nearby.

202

On the right you come to a crofthouse and, further right, a ruined one. Between the two and over a pasture, lies the largest burnt mound in Shetland, 128 feet by 89 feet and almost 10 feet high.

Stride on along the narrow road between the sheep pastures and the occasional tethered cow, where the verges are bright with daisies, buttercups, silver weed, plantains and white clover. Where the road divides, take the left fork to pass the well-equipped school, which caters for pupils until they are 11 years old. Beside the school is the community hall. Here you can enjoy the various activities, including a weekly workshop of the Fair Isle Crafts Co-operative.

Head on along the road to visit the beautifully refurbished Church of Scotland kirk, built in 1892. Close by, on its hill and installed in 1982, is an aerogenerator, which helps supply electricity for the isle. Because of the expense, current is supplied for only part of the day, with more in winter.

Continue on where blue squill covers the pasture to visit the Methodist chapel, another lovely quiet haven. Services alternate between the two churches, most people attending both. Behind the church is the old school building, which houses the George Waterston memorial centre and museum. The first school on the island was erected around 1730 and later moved to this site until the present school was built in 1882. From then on it was the home of the community hall until 1980. It now houses the archives, photographs and artefacts of Fair Isle's past, some inspiring and some depressing.

Stride on down the road to the immaculately kept walled graveyard where there is a sunny bench seat. The wall behind was once part of an older kirk. Some of the headstones make for sad reading. Look for the iron cross to the right of the gate which commemorates the wreck, in 1588, of *El Gran Grifon,* flagship of the defeated Armada. More than 300 survivors were landed on the isle to be supported by 17 households living at subsistence level. Over 50 of the Spaniards died of starvation. In 1984 the Spanish came again to dedicate the cross in the kirkyard.

Continue along the road, through the gate, to pass the Puffinn, an old fish store, since 1976 a hostel used by school-children and people from the observatory. Here on the shore sheep feed on seaweed.

Nearby are old boat nousts and flat stones for drying fish. Here, too, is South Haven pier, which has to be approached past skerries and small stacks — rather more perilous than the North Haven harbour. Male eiders congregate in large packs, house martins skim over the seaweed and seals disport.

Return past the Puffinn to visit the taller South Light, which has a brilliant white-and-yellow accommodation block. Return along the road and, where it divides, keep to the left branch. Climb the hill to pass a crofthouse with an old kiln used for drying corn and oats. In the workshop on the croft spinning wheels are repaired and made. Keep climbing to the well-stocked shop, where you can buy postcards, and there is a toilet.

Continue along the road, remembering to take the left turn to the airstrip.

Fair Isle Airstrip

Other books by Mary Welsh available from the Westmorland Gazette:

A Naturalist's Guide to
Lakeland Waterfalls throughout the year —
Southern Lakeland

A Second Naturalist's Guide to
Lakeland Waterfalls throughout the year —
North West Lakeland

A Third Naturalist's Guide to
Lakeland Waterfalls throughout the year —
North East Lakeland

A Fourth Naturalist's Guide to
Lakeland Waterfalls throughout the year —
covering all of Lakeland

Forty-four Walks on the Isle of Arran

Walks on the Isle of Skye

Walks in Wester Ross

Walks in Perthshire

Walks in the Western Isles

Walks in Orkney